LET'S GO FOSSIL SHARK TOOTH HUNTING

A GUIDE FOR IDENTIFYING SHARKS AND WHERE AND HOW
TO FIND THEIR SUPERBLY FORMED FOSSILIZED TEETH

by

B. Clay Cartmell

Eighth Printing March, 1993

NATURAL SCIENCE RESEARCH

A Search Series Book Venice, Florida

LET'S GO FOSSIL SHARK TOOTH HUNTING

Library of Congress Catalog Card Number 76-26369

ISBN 0-930498-01-1

Published by .... Natural Science Research,
2307 Manchester Road,
Ann Arbor, Michigan 48104

Printed and bound in the United States of America

CONTENTS

COVER

Reconstruction of a Carcharodon megalodon's jaws.

Courtesy of the
American Museum of Natural History
New York, New York

Illustrations by the author

PREFACE

Shark! Probably no other creature on the face of the Earth is so feared by man as the shark. In the relatively brief time mankind has been a coinhabitant with them on this planet, the shark has been almost universally looked upon as a mortal enemy. Yet it is man who is the only natural enemy of sharks. In their own element, these creatures have nothing else to fear except each other. They have ruled without serious challenge this major part of the Earth's surface for at least 150 million years. But as man has feared these swift, graceful predators of the sea, so has he held them in great awe and respect. They are fascinating, deadly, efficient creatures that have little changed since the time of the great dinosaur die-off more than 60 million years ago. Even their ancestors, dating back over 300 million years ago, had many of the physical characteristics still apparent in today's sea dwellers. And bearing evidence to their past existence has been the vast quantities of hard, durable, superbly crafted teeth that have been found in fossil deposits throughout the world. They are far more abundant than is generally known. Besides the many millions that have been found in the past, large numbers continue to be collected daily in known fossil-rich locations. Using proven collecting techniques described in this book and working favorable sites such as the beaches at Venice, Florida, it is almost certain an observant hunter can find fossil shark teeth.

Just as the shark itself is a fascinating attraction, so is fossil tooth hunting. It's an immensely enjoyable out-of-doors recreational activity; it's an addictive pastime! But it is by no means just the assortment of attractive fossil teeth that intrigues the many people who participate in this hobby. It's also the surf-smoothed dark sand beaches, the ever-changing sea and the clean, fresh ocean air. It's the color of the sky, the noise of the waves and the taste of the wind. It's these things and many more that help form the addiction. Fossil tooth collectors are captured as much by the environment they hunt in as by the hunt itself.

As many first-time hunters have discovered, some coastline beaches are devoid of any fossilized shark's teeth. But even along shore lines known to be productive, these ancient remnants of the past are generally to be found in just a limited number of places. Tides and weather conditions often play a major role in their location. Unfortunately, many beginners become discouraged and give up before they have learned when and where they should look along these beaches. Those who are attuned to these factors consistently find sizeable numbers of attractive fossil specimens.

While most who have never tried this type of collecting are extremely skeptical that such many-million-year-old fossils even exist, much less in any significant quantities, hundreds of these ancient relics of the past are collected nearly every day of the year along Florida's west coast and elsewhere in this country. But as in most other forms of hunting and collecting, the majority of these small, dark, gracefully shaped teeth are found by those who know where to look and under what conditions. That's what this book is about. It's to help those interested in finding these fossils and identifying them by shark species.

Besides having collected many thousands of these fascinating relics myself, I've had the opportunity to talk at length with many of the veteran beach-prowlers who consistently bring in outstandingly large jewelry-grade tooth specimens. In the time they spend at it, they invariably seem to have far better results than the vast majority of other hunters. It isn't just luck. It involves a great deal of know-how! As much as possible, their observations and advice are reflected in this book.

In addition to the beach hunters, grateful acknowledgement must also be given to the researchers, marine biologists, paleontologists and geologists who have so painstakingly pieced together the story of our planet and its life forms since its creation some 3 or 4 billion years ago. Among the creatures they have studied have been the sharks. It has been in a large part from this fish's fossilized teeth that scientists have been able to trace the evolution of these creatures in the ever-changing seas of the world. It is sobering indeed to realize that members of the shark family first appeared as a life form over 300 million years ago, while man's ancestors date back a mere 3 million.

After you have read this book, you too should be able to find many of these intriguing, gracefully formed prehistoric teeth which are so abundant along some coast lines. And although this book is written about the Venice, Florida beaches, most of the fossil shark tooth hunting methods mentioned here are equally applicable to coastal and inland fossil beds elsewhere in this country.

No matter where it may be, understanding the various beach and sea conditions that are most favorable for fossil hunting should improve the results of your search effort. Read, observe, then hunt. And good luck! I hope to see you on the beckoning beach.

B. Clay Cartmell
Venice, Florida

SHARKS DOWN THROUGH THE AGES

In many of the large museums of natural history throughout the world, the fossilized skeletal reconstructions of the great dinosaurs of the past tower over the awed spectators who marvel at their life-like structure (Figure 1). These creatures reached lengths of over 80 feet and weights of more than 50 tons. Their well-preserved bones have been recovered from the ancient beds of sediment where these huge creatures perished millions and millions of years ago. But these same museums contain no similar reconstructions of the awesomely large sharks that prowled the ancient seas during and after the time of the dinosaurs. When these sharks passed away, they left no bones to be fossilized. There have been no well-preserved skeletal frames to tell man of their size and of their shape.

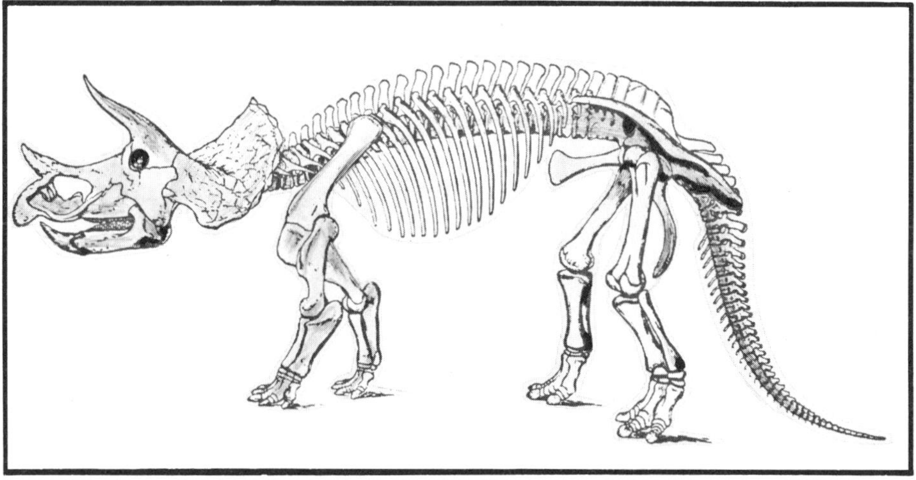

Figure 1.

Unlike most other large members of the animal kingdom, the graceful, powerful-jawed, often aggressive sharks do not have a bony skeleton. Instead, their structure is of a firm, flexible but relatively quickly decomposed cartilage. Consequently when a shark dies, its skeleton usually disintegrates before it has time to fossilize in the same manner as bone. The gristle-like spine, fins, jaws and other structural parts waste away much in the same way as the dead creature's lifeless skin and flesh. This is not true of most other fishes, which have bony skeletons, nor of the great mammals of the sea, such as the whales, porpoises, walruses and sea lions. When these creatures' prehistoric ancestors passed away, some of their skeletal bones were buried in beds of sediment where they were fossilized to bear witness to their former existence (Figure 2). But in the over 300 million years that sharks have been in existence, they have had softer, less easily preserved cartilage-like skeletons.

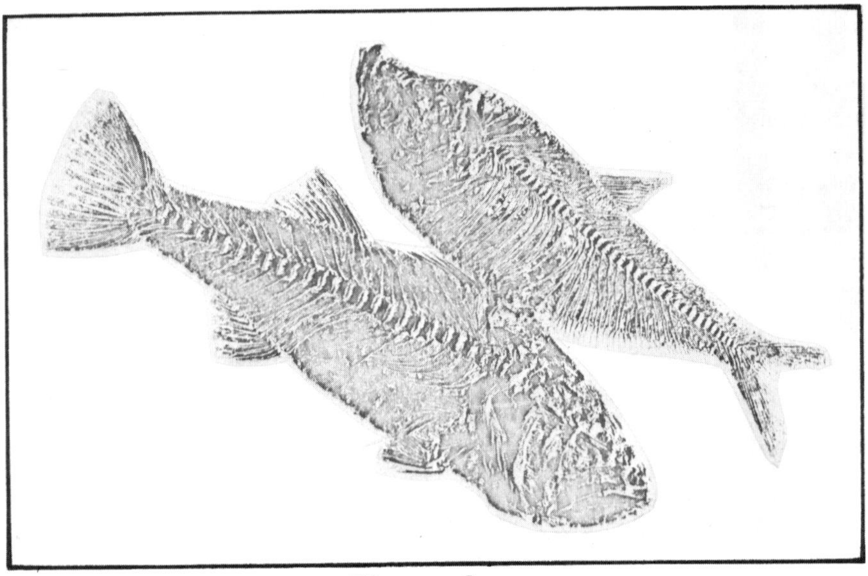

Figure 2.

Fortunately for marine biologists and paleontologists, sharks do have one long-lasting, durable appendage to tell of their past existence and size: their tough, efficient teeth. For most members of the animal kingdom, teeth are the most durable tissue in the body. But for the cartilage-framed sharks, these - and to a much lesser extent a few fin spines and skin denticles (small tooth-like enamel projections in the skin) - are generally the only remaining trace of their former presence. Vast numbers of these hard, dense, bony teeth have been found in sea-bottom deposits dating back millions and millions of years. These teeth have helped to trace this crea-

ture's evolution since its first appearance on the earth.
There have, fortunately, been other infrequent but extremely important finds. Picture-like fossil imprints of the very earliest of these fish have been found in deposits where the fish's body was covered before it completely decomposed. Such print-like outlines have provided an invaluable insight as to just what these ancient sea dwellers looked like. At one such place near the center of the State of Montana called Bear Gulch, new fossil finds continue to be made even today.

Fossil Shark Teeth

Once submerged under the shallow, warm sea that stretched across western North America for 600 miles during part of the Carboniferous period, Bear Gulch has proven to be a virtual treasure of shark skeletal remains. Scientists believe that rapid sedimentation in this part of the ancient sea quickly buried many dead sharks before they had broken up or decomposed beyond recognition. From this gulch's slabs of sharply layered soft limestone, beautifully preserved skeletons have been found embedded inside. To date, 64 shark species have been found, many previously unknown. Some have been so well preserved that the remains of shrimp can be seen in their stomachs. And these ancient members of today's shark family have been found in every size and shape fitting dozens of ecological niches. Included have been the fossils of "unicorn sharks" with spikes growing out of the tops of their heads, flat-shaped sharks resembling flounders, sharks with enlarged pectoral fins that enabled them to leap out of the water and glide, sharks with crablike claws on their snouts and tiny sharks only an inch and a quarter long. One, a four-foot-long creature, had a dorsal fin hinged like the rudder on the tail of an airplane. This ancient creature, by swinging the movable aft portion of its dorsal fin, could turn on a dime and easily out-maneuver any of today's sharks which have almost totally rigid dorsal fins.

Numerous other inland sites have also provided image-like imprints of today's sharks ancestors. One of the best of these likenesses was taken from Upper Devonian shales south of Lake Erie. Dating back over 250 million years, this nearly perfect preservation of a less-than-three-feet-long fish shows in remarkable detail the anatomy of the ancient specimen. From fossil records such as these, paleontologists have found that in many respects some sharks of the past bore a remarkable similarity to those of today. This creature has fit its ecological niche so well that it has been able to maintain its position with little change in physical characteristics over the hundreds of millions of years it has been on earth.

From what scientists have been able to reconstruct of this earth's past, the first primitive fish - the ostracodermis - appeared in the Early Ordovician seas over 400 million years ago (Table I). It wasn't, however, until nearly 100 million years later in deposits of the Middle Devonian period that the first shark remains appeared. They were found where the sea once flooded much of the midwestern part of the United States.

GEOLOGIC TIME CHART

TABLE I

ERA	PERIOD	EPOCH	MILLIONS OF YEARS AGO	IMPORTANT EVENTS
CENOZOIC	QUARTERNARY	RECENT	0-2	Glaciers melted; continents high. Early types of mammals die out.
		PLEISTOCENE		Four great glacial advances; mountains continue to rise. Carcharodon megalodon becomes extinct.
	TERTIARY	PLIOCENE	2-12	World-wide uplifts and mountain building; there is a reduction in number of shark species.
		MIOCENE	12-28	Sierra Nevada and Rockies uplifted; lands are high and dry. Modern whales and other sea mammals appear.
		OLIGOCENE	28-40	Lands are low and moist; mammals become gigantic in size. Alps and Himalayas begin to rise.
		EOCENE	40-70	
		PALEOCENE		Seas are narrow; mountains are high then worn down by erosion. Dinosaurs are extinct; sharks are dominant predators of the seas.
MESOZOIC	CRETACEOUS		70-130	Last great spread of seas; most of existing shark families appear by the close of period. Dinosaurs suddenly died out.
	JURASSIC		130-165	Dinosaurs dominate; seas are widespread. Modernized shark families begin to appear.
	TRIASSIC		165-200	Continents generally high; land dry in many regions. Sharks adapt and increase; many reptiles.
PALEOZOIC	PERMIAN		200-230	Continents raised; extensive glaciation. Shark species greatly reduced.
	CARBONIFEROUS		230-285	Seas spread and withdraw many times; first reptiles appear later in period. Many coal forming swamps.
	DEVONIAN		285-340	Much land covered by seas; sharks evolve. Many armored fish.
	SILURIAN		340-380	Seas are widespread. First air-breathing animals appear (probably similar to scorpions or lungfish).
	ORDOVICIAN		380-460	Over 60% of North America covered by sea; fish with backbones first appear. Climate very warm.
	CAMBRIAN		460-550	All animals lived in the oceans and none had backbones. Shellfish and snails appeared.
PRECAMBRIAN			550-3500	Earth's crust is solidified; many rocks and minerals formed. Very simple life forms appear later in period (such as worms, jellyfish & algae).

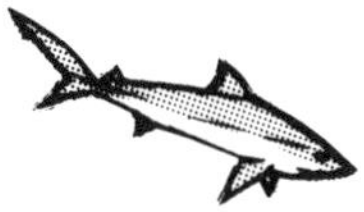

While some authorities contend that even earlier shark forms probably existed in the mid-Silurian period, there is little physical evidence to support this position. Those who do not agree with this earlier date say it is difficult to believe that the teeth of any supposedly earlier forms have escaped scientific attention. In fact, they have concluded that the absence of fossil shark teeth in Silurian strata suggests that sharks are degenerate rather than primitive, that somewhere along the line after the earliest fish had risen from their obscure freshwater origin and taken to the sea, sharks lost their ability to form bones and became separated from the bony fishes.

These first primitive members of the shark family flourished until sometime near the end of the Paleozoic. Then, for some unexplained reason, most of them disappeared. So did many mammals and other marine invertebrates, some of which were undoubtedly the shark's prey. Some scientists speculate that a natural disaster, such as a severe climatic change, may have been the cause. It occurred so abruptly that some creatures died out before they had time to adapt to the new environment. Others, however, suggest yet another reason. They believe the evolution of the more advanced bony fishes drove many forms of sharks to extinction. They simply couldn't continue to compete.

Not all sharks, however, perished. Many shark-like fishes once again populated the seas during the latter part of the Mesozoic era. This was also a period of

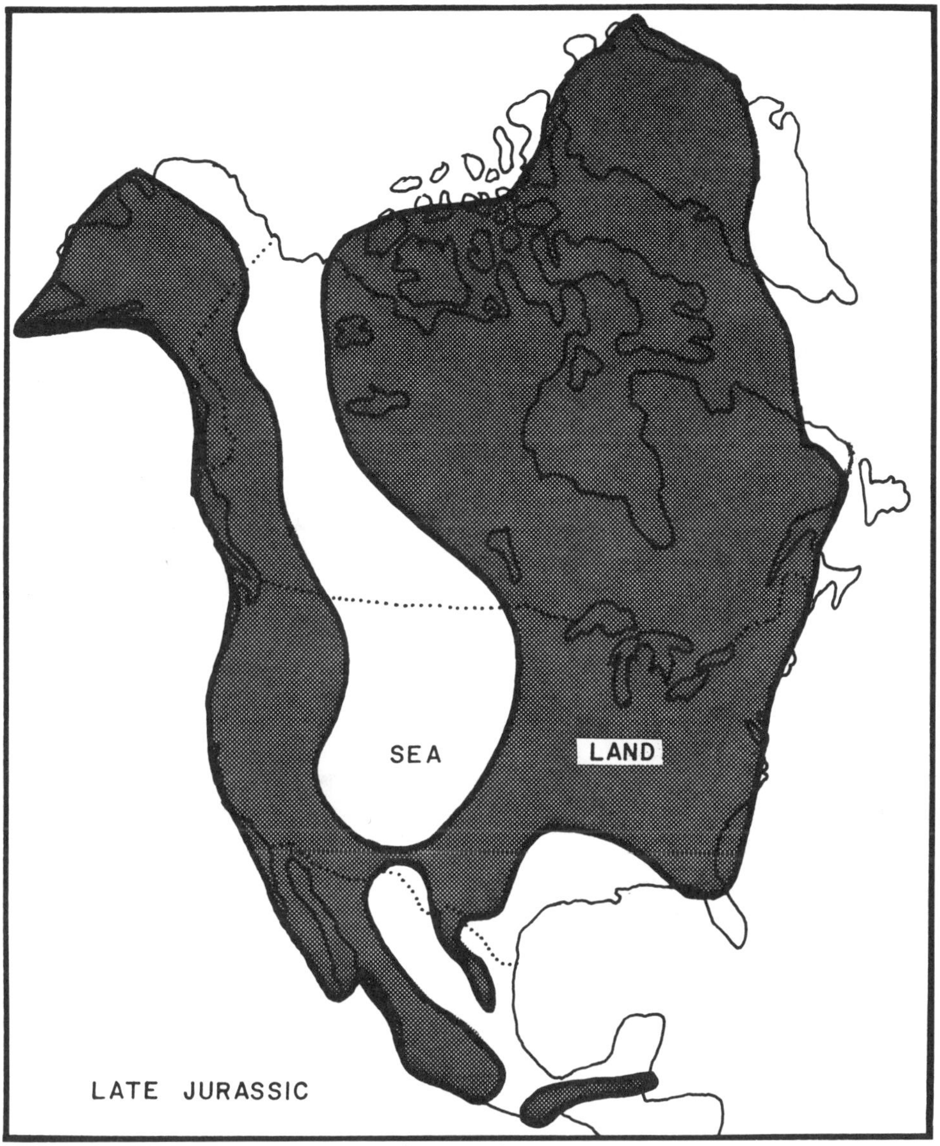

Figure 3.

numerous bony fishes. During both the Mesozoic and later Cenozoic, many parts of what are now the continents of the world were partially or completely submerged by the seas. Florida was no exception. It was submerged and emerged repeatedly. In the late Jurassic period, for example, most of the State was covered by water (Fig-

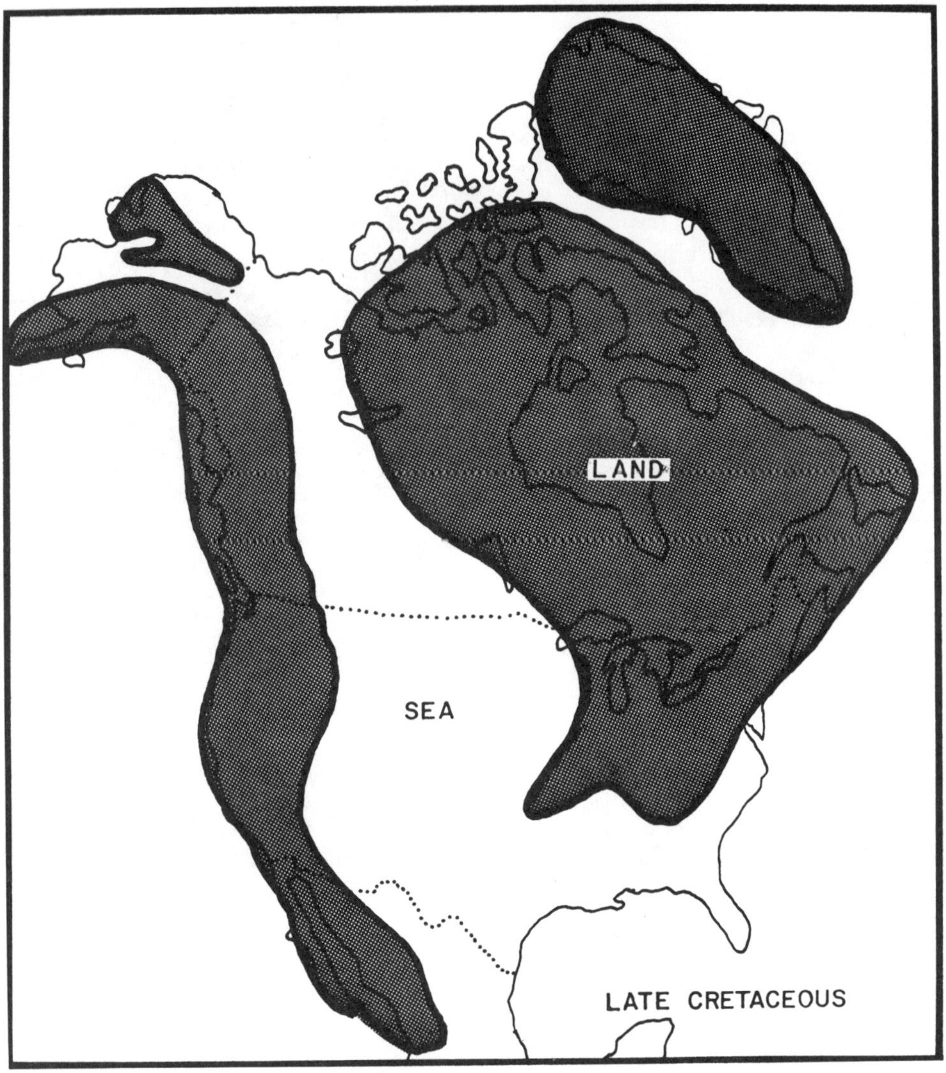

Figure 4.

ure 3). During this same period, the "modernized" phase of shark development began. A rapid deployment then continued throughout the succeeding Cretaceous period (Figure 4). With the exception of the Hammerheads which first appeared about 25 million years ago, most of the dozen or more families of sharks found in our seas today had evolved by the end of this period. For example, the fossil teeth of the Mackerel shark family date back to early Cretaceous deposits. Represented by such modern-day fish as the Mako and Great White, sharks of this family have populated the seas of the world for over 100 million years.

As the Cretaceous period ended and the Tertiary started, the great reptilian dinosaurs unexplainably passed from the scene. Some type of natural disaster may have occurred and these great "thunder lizards" vanished from the face of the earth. But not the sharks. As attested to by the abundance of their fossil remains in Tertiary period deposits, these creatures continued to flourish. In fact, with the passing of the dinosaurs, sharks became the dominant predators in the seas of the world. They continue in this role even today. In the main, it takes a shark to kill a shark, and sharks do eat sharks. During the 70 million years of the Tertiary period, major changes continued to occur in the earth's surface. Great masses of rock were uplifted to form the North American Rockies and the Sierra Nevada mountains. The continent-sized land masses, or Tectonic "plates," continued to drift further apart (Figure 5). The gap widened between Europe and North America and between Africa and South America. Throughout this calendar of events, the sharks

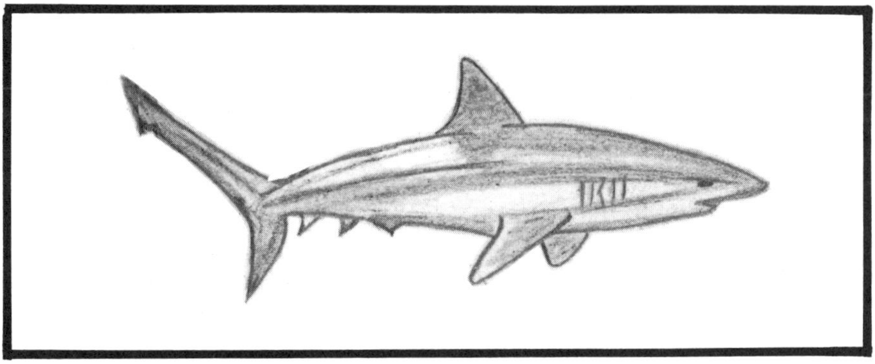

continued to flourish. When they died, their remains settled into the ever-deepening sea bottom deposits. There they continued to be buried under the accumulated sediments of the millions and millions of years of the sea's evolution. But the sea floors themselves did not remain unchanged during these monumental, earth-reshaping events. Great internal forces within the earth shoved parts of these ancient marine beds high above sea

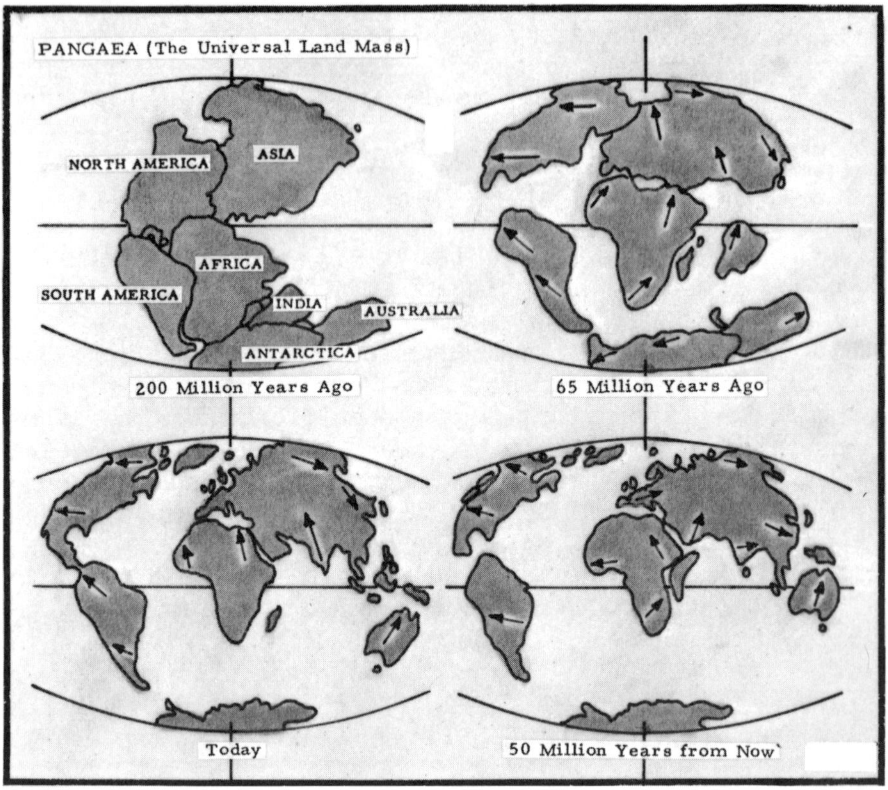

Figure 5.

level. The earth's polar ice caps also changed, growing in size at the expense of the seas. Submerged lands once again emerged as the seas retreated.

It has been from both these elevated, no longer submerged sea bottom deposits as well as the ocean floor itself that paleontologists have been able effectively to identify and to trace the life cycles of the creatures that lived in the seas of the past. The fossil remains in the different layers of these former sea floor sediments have made it possible for researchers to reconstruct what life must have been like in the ancient seas. As the fossilized remains of various creatures either first appeared or dropped from sight, scientists have been able to determine from these geologically dated sediments for approximately what span of time each species has filled a niche in the earth's animal kingdom. For the sharks, it has been their fossilzied teeth that have told of their presence, their evolution and their passing in the seas of the world. They have identified the presence of new species and the passing of others. They have been invaluable in tracing the slow evolutionary changes in the different shark families over the eons of time. Nevertheless, it has taken careful study, expert analysis and a vast accumulation of scientific observations to piece together this story. Even with this background, it is still sometimes next to impossible to identify positively a single isolated shark's tooth as belonging to a single shark species. Too many have teeth that look very much alike. Often the best that can be said is that the tooth is from any one of several possible species.

Fossil Shark Teeth

Identifying the age of a tooth specimen is yet another often insurmountable task. Most commonly, the dating of a fossil is established by the age of the earthen deposits from which it is taken. An undisturbed tooth dug from known Miocene deposits, for example, is identified as being at least 12 to 28 million years old. If the fossil is found in the upper part of these deposits, it is assumed to be closer to the 12 million figure. On the other hand, if it is from near the bottom, it is believed to be approaching the 28 million level. But when a fossil tooth is found washed up on a beach or is taken from shifting sea bottom deposits, it is nearly impossible to say with any certainty what its age might be. In a few cases, known evolutionary changes in the teeth themselves may help date the specimen, despite the lack of burial site information. But for most sharks this is not a factor. Their teeth have undergone little in the way of modifications over the vast period of time they have been in existence.

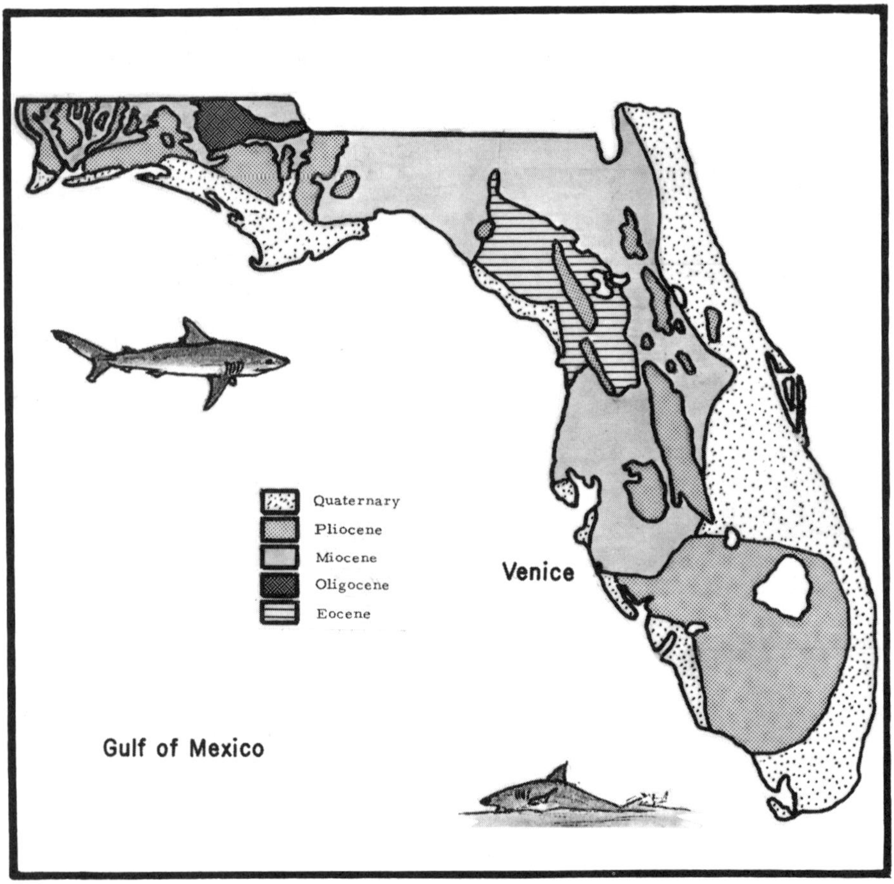

Figure 6.

When a fossil tooth is found along the seashore, the best that can often be said about it is that it is no older than the sedimentary deposits from which it came. If, for instance, the deposits are of Miocene origin, then it can be reasonably assumed that the tooth specimen is no more than 28 million years old. It may by much younger. It must be remembered that over the ensuing millions of years, vast numbers of additional fish, including sharks, also perished in the same area. Their remains, including their teeth, also settled to the bottom, where they too were buried. When the shifting shallow-water sea bottom uncovered the former Miocene deposits, it also freed any fossils buried in the younger overlying sediments. Consequently, all that can usually be said about a fossil tooth found under these circumstances is that it might have come from the oldest sedimentary layers. Figure 6 shows the geological age of the exposed land surface in Florida.

As would be expected, scientists have constantly been in search of other more direct and positive methods for age dating the fossil remains of once living creatures. Except for the Carbon 14 method, which is applicable to objects less than 40,000 years old, no successful technique has yet been found. Outward appearances, for ex-

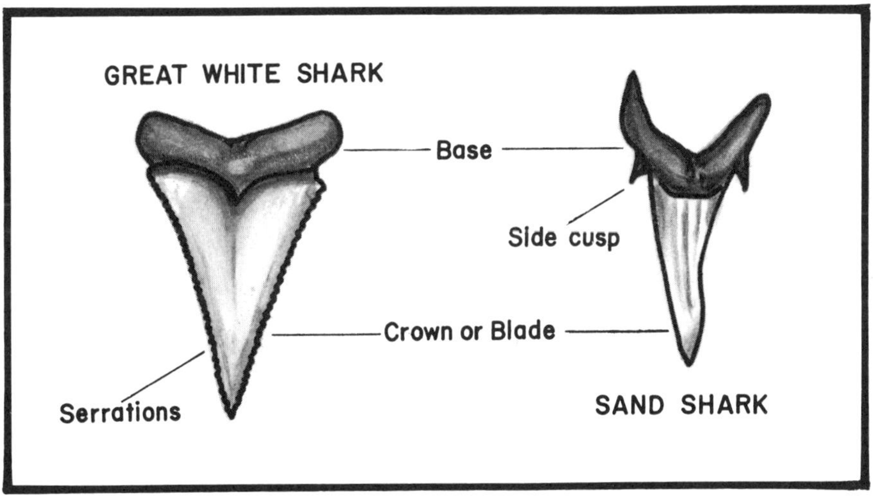

Figure 7.

ample, are generally of little help. An extremely ancient shark's tooth that has been recently freed from its burial may show little in the way of wear. Details, such as edge serrations and side cusps (Figure 7), may be so clearly defined that the tooth appears to have been recently removed from a living creature. On the other hand, a fossil of relatively recent origin that has been continuously scraped along the sea bottom may appear to be extremely old.

While the modern Carbon 14 measuring technique has proven to be an extremely accurate and useful method for dating the remains of formerly living creatures of relatively recent origin, its effectiveness is confined to objects less than 40,000 years old. It works on the principle that a known percent of carbon in every living creature is in the form of the isotope Carbon 14. Through a natural process, this radioactive isotope disintegrates into nitrogen. The rate at which it does so is not influenced by external terrestrial conditions. In a living creature, the carbon that is lost in this manner is constantly replenished. But when death occurs, replenishment stops and all of the carbon is ultimately lost. The Carbon 14 "clock" gradually begins to run down by giving off beta particles and reverting to nitrogen. It is very much like the old-fashioned hour glass which "tells" time by the passage of sand from one compartment to the other. In the case of the Carbon 14 "clock", it takes about 40,000 years for the remaining radioactive isotopes to reach such a low level that they can no longer be measured.

One misconception some collectors have about the age of a fossil tooth concerns its color. Light colors are considered to represent more recent fossils and dark shades, more ancient ones. This, however, is not necessarily true. Though the teeth of living and recently deceased sharks tend toward a white color, they are not fossilized. Fossil teeth take on their color from the environment in which they were buried. Color is imparted to a tooth through a combination of the surrounding earth and vegetation. While the original enamel is not replaced by minerals, as often happens with bone, the tooth itself does become color-stained.

For fossils found in the Venice, Florida area, this coloration ranges from a dark, almost ebony black to a light, relatively pale shade of brown. Generally, a tooth or bone is classified as a fossil if it is 10,000 years or older.

ANIMAL KINGDOM

(PHYLUM CHORDATA - SUBPHYLUM VERTEBRATA)

- SUPERCLASS PIECES:	Aquatic vertebrates
. CLASS AGNATHA:	Jawless fishes
. CLASS PLACODERM:	(extinct)
. CLASS CHONORICHTHYES:	sharks, rays
. CLASS OSTEICTHYES:	bony fishes, such as sturgeon, trout, perch, etc.
- SUPERCLASS TETRAPODA:	Land vertebrates
. CLASS AMPHIBIA:	frogs, toads
. CLASS REPTILIA:	lizards, snakes, alligators
. CLASS AVES:	birds
. CLASS MAMMALIA:	monkeys, men, dogs, cats, whales, elephants, horses, cows, etc.

CLASSIFICATION OF THE CHONDRICHTHYES
(ELASMOBRANCHS OR CARTILAGINOUS FISHES)

- SUBCLASS SELACHII	All recent and fossil sharks and rays
. SUPERORDER PROTOSELACHII	Protoselachians or fossil sharklike forms
. SUPERORDER EUSELACHII	Selachians, i.e. all modern sharks and rays
- ORDER PLEUROTREMATA	SHARKS (i.e. sharks, dogfishes, hounds, topes, etc.)
- ORDER HYPOTREMATA	RAYS (i.e. skates, rays, torpedoes, etc.)
- SUBCLASS BRADYODONTI	CHIMAERAS Ratfishes

TABLE II

THE SHARKS

While marine biologists have identified over 250 different species of sharks in today's ocean, far fewer are to be found with any regularity off the Eastern and Gulf coasts of the United States. Of these, probably less than a dozen are the source of the vast majority of fossil shark's teeth found on the Venice, Florida and other Gulf coast beaches. But besides the fossil teeth of these extant species, those of several extinct sharks are also collected. Most are from just five deceased members of this fish family. So in total, less than twenty living and extinct species are the source of nearly all of the fossilized shark's teeth found in and around Venice, Florida.

In the orderly, scientific classification of all members of the animal kingdom, sharks are included in the class of aquatic vertebrates called Chonorichthyes. These are elasmobranches or cartilaginous fishes, as opposed to bony fishes (Table II). Under the sub-class Selachii, modern sharks fall in the order Pleurotemata. The families within this order and their more common names are listed in Table III. They range from the midwater (dwarf) shark (Squaliolus laticaudus), which matures at about

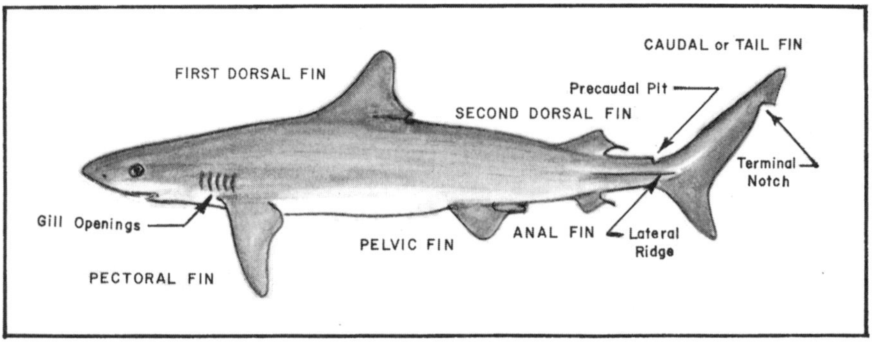

Figure 8.

6" to 8", to the multi-ton, probably over-60-feet-long Whale shark. Of the over 250 species, 27 are considered

ORDER PLEUROTREMATA

	Common Name	Principal Genera
SUBORDER HEXANCHIFORMES		
. Family HEXANCHIDAE	Cow Sharks Combtoothed, Six-or Seven-gilled Sharks	Hexanchus Heptranchias Notorhynchus
. Family CHLAMYDOSELACHIDAE	Frilled Sharks	Chlamydoselachus
SUBORDER HETERODONTIFORMES		
. Family HETERODONTIDAE	Port Jackson Sharks, Horn Sharks or Bull-headed Sharks	Heterodontus 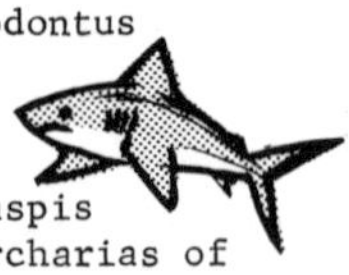
SUBORDER GALEIFORMES		
. Family ODONTASPIDIDAE (formerly Carchariidae)	Sand Sharks	Odontaspis (= Carcharias of authors)
. Family SCAPANORHYNCHIDAE	Goblin Sharks	Mitsukurina (fossil-genus Scapanorhyn-chus)
. Family ISURIDAE 	Mackerel Sharks	Carcharodon, Isurus Lamna
. Family CETORHINIDAE	Basking Sharks	Cetorhinus
. Family ALOPIIDAE	Thresher Sharks	Alopias
. Family ORECTOLOBIDAE	Carpet Sharks	Orectolobus Ginglymostoma Stegostoma
. Family RHINCODONTIDAE	Whale Sharks	Rhincodon
. Family SCYLIORHINIDAE	Dogfishes, Cat Sharks, Swell Sharks	Scyliorhinus, Galeus Apristurus Cephaloscylium
. Family PSEUDOTRIAKIDAE	False Cat Sharks	Pseudotriakis
. Family TRIAKIDAE (formerly Galeorhinidae)	Smooth Hounds or Smooth Dogfishes	Triakis, Mustelus Triaenodon
. Family CARCHARHINIDAE	Grey Sharks Requiem Sharks 	Carcharhinus Negaprion, Prionace, Galeocerdo, Scoliodon, Galeorhinus, Hemipristis
. Family SPHYRNIDAE	Hammerhead Sharks	Sphyrna
SUBORDER SQUALIFORMES		
. Family SQUALIDAE	Spiny Dogfishes	Squalus, Etmopterus Centroscymnus Oxynotus, Centrophorus
. Family DALATIIDAE	Sleeper Sharks Spineless Dogfishes	Somniosus, Isistius, Euprotomicrus, Squaliolus, Dalatius
. Family ECHINORHINIDAE	Bramble Sharks	Echinorhinus
. Family PRISTIOPHORIDAE	Saw Sharks	Pristiophorus, Pliotrema
. Family SQUATINIDAE	Monkfishes, Angel Sharks	Squatina

TABLE III

dangerous to man.

Few things about the shark are universally true, so varied are sharks among themselves. Their bonelessness, nevertheless, is one important difference between them and most other fishes. For a predator like the shark, this has its advantages. Cartilage is lighter than bone. This helps offset the shark's lack of an air bladder which most fish have for buoyancy. Consequently when preying on other fish, a shark can change depths rapidly without risking fatal injury. The shark's cartilage spine also extends into the generally long upper lobe of its tail increasing its swimming strength.

But besides their unique internal structure, sharks do have several other more observable physical characteristics which help to identify them (Figure 8). They have from 5 to 7 gill slits on each side of the head which open separately to the outside of the body. Except for a few species with more flattened forms, most sharks have torpedo-like bodies. Many also have high-standing first dorsal fins, coupled with a broad, powerful tail fin. These fins differ in many respects from those of the bony fish, the most apparent being that they are covered by the same skin as the body. Another difference is that they can't be flattened against the body like most other fishes.

Most sharks have well developed jaws and bony teeth. Most are scavengers, although not totally dependent upon this means of obtaining food. As far as is known, all are carnivores.

For the fossil tooth hunter, it is this fish's powerful jaws and efficient teeth that are of the greatest interest. In sharks, the dental structure is distinct from that of most other living vertebrates. Sharks have several rows of replacement teeth, usually from five to as many as 16 rows, already partially in place not far behind their functional ones. Just behind the visible front teeth, these reserve rows are usually one on top of the other flattened beneath a thin membrane. Should a front, functional tooth be lost for any reason, a replacement moves forward shortly thereafter. In the normal course of a shark's life, it is believed such losses occur quite frequently. In fact some believe a few species may grow a whole new set of teeth at least once every year. Experiments with living Lemon sharks have shown a lost tooth is replaced in less than 10 days. Based on yet other data collected on Tiger sharks, it has been estimated that an average sized fish of this species may produce well over 20,000 teeth in a 10-year life span. During the underwater filming of huge 14-foot and larger man-eating Great White sharks off the coast of Australia, divers reported seeing teeth break loose from the jaws of these huge creatures as they seized part of the steel bar cages protecting the photographers. One observer said the white teeth fluttering downward in the water looked like a "rain of popcorn." Although a Great White has never been kept alive in captivity long enough to make any lengthy firsthand observations, such lost teeth undoubtedly are replaced in a relatively short time.

In most sharks, the replacement rows of teeth are not functional; only the erect front ones are. There are, however, exceptions. In the Nurse shark, for instance, two or three series may be in use simultaneously.

In a broad sense, a shark's tooth is composed of a "base" and a "crown" (Figure 9). The surface of the

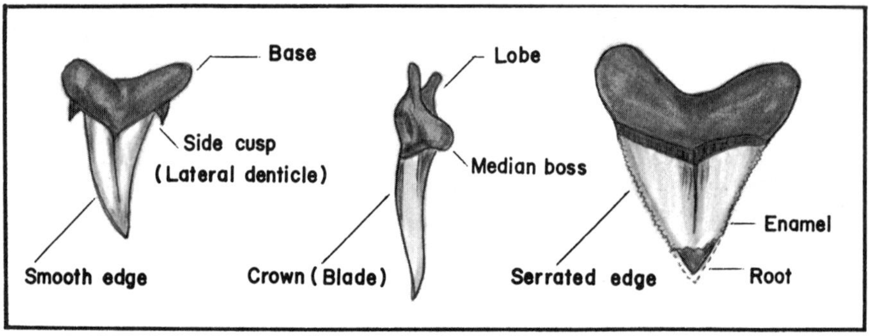

Figure 9.

"crown" is covered by an enamel which is considerably denser than the remainder of the tooth. This hard, structureless cap usually covers an inside core called the "root." It is most often composed of a form of dentine. The bony "base" of the tooth is not rooted in the fish's jaw. Unlike mammals, they are attached by a strong, flexible collagen-rich sheath of connective tissue.

Also unlike many other creatures, the shark's upper jaw is not fused to the cranium. As a result of this loose but strong and flexible connection, some sharks can actually open their mouths until their snouts are practically perpendicular.

In sharks, the teeth in one jaw are not necessarily identical with those in the other. Those in the upper sometimes differ in both shape and appearance from those in the lower. But be it upper or lower, the configuration of the teeth in either jaw remains very nearly the same, except that they usually become progressively smaller toward the corners of the mouth.

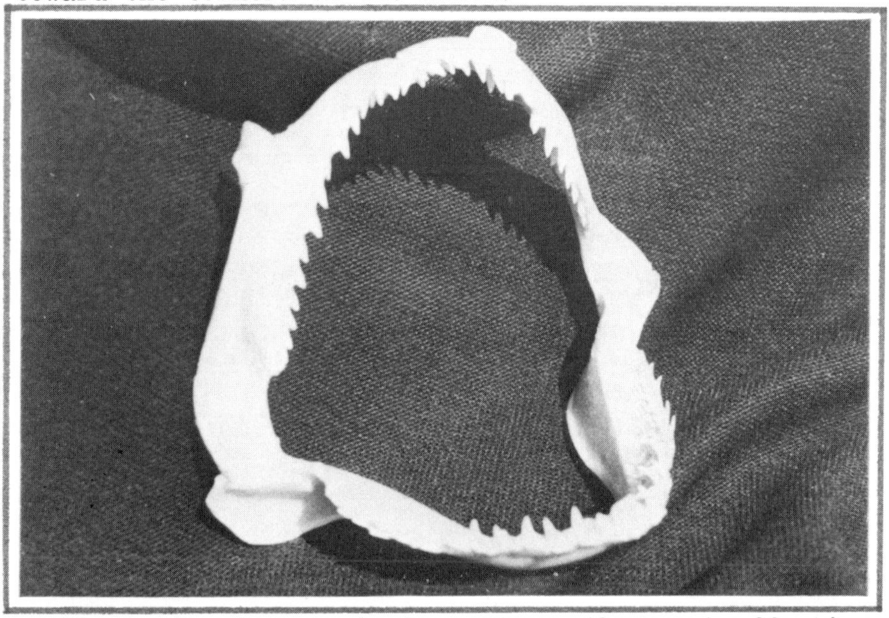

The teeth of some sharks rank as the most effective cutting instruments known in nature. They are remarkably efficient. While a big cat such as a lion or tiger may struggle with its kill for hours, a shark of similar size could cut the same prey in two with a single snap of its jaw. You or I using a sharp knife, the leverage of our arm and our superior intellect might spend several minutes cutting a five to ten pound fish in half. A shark our size can do it in less than a second! At the Mote Marine Laboratory, the bite pressure of an eight foot Dusky shark has been measured at over 18 tons per square inch at the tips of its teeth. With this in mind, just imagine what force a huge 15 to 20-foot Great White shark might bring to bear when it clamps down on a victim!

Of the shark family members considered, the Atlantic Sand (both living and extinct species), the Bull, the Lemon, the Tiger (both living and extinct species), the Dusky, the Blacktip, the Spinner, the Brown, the Hammerhead, the Mako (both living and extinct species) and the Great White (both living and the extinct Carcharodon megalodon) are the source of practically all of the fossilized shark's teeth found in the Venice, Florida region. Information, nevertheless, has been included on a few others of the large better-known shark species that frequent the seas of the world: the Blue, Thresher, Whitetip, Whale, Porbeagle and Nurse.

ATLANTIC SAND SHARK (Caracharias taurus) Figure 10.

This is a fairly common coastal-water shark which lives near the bottom close to the shore. A pale gray-brown on the upper surface of its body running to a gray-white on the belly, it customarily has yellow-brown oval or round spots on its sides, caudal and dorsal fins. Generally sluggish in nature, it feeds mainly on small fish, crabs and squid, often in less than 6 feet of water. It reaches lengths of about 10 feet and weights of as much as 400 pounds. A mature fish is generally

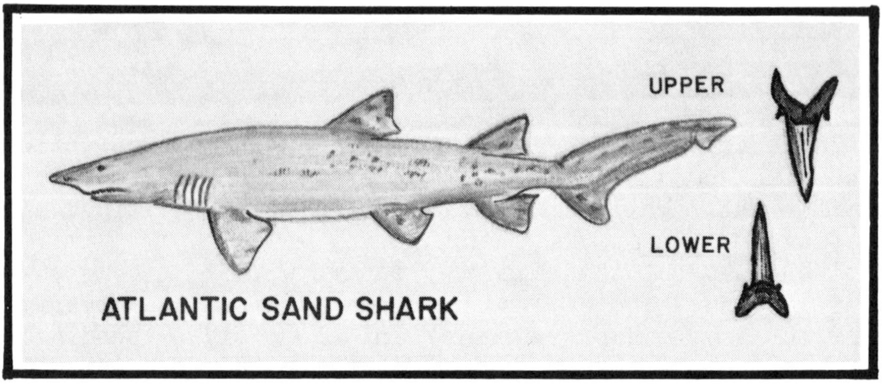

Figure 10.

over 7 feet long. It has been implicated in attacks on man.

Among collectors, the long, gracefully curved, fang-like fossil teeth of this shark are considered to be the most attractive of all specimens. Instead of having sharp cutting edges, the teeth of the Sand shark are spike-shaped to impale their prey. They are an excellent example of adaptation of tooth form to feeding habits.

From a size standpoint, any Sand shark tooth longer than 1-1/2 inches is an exceptionally large one. The teeth in this shark's upper and lower jaw are very similar in appearance. There is a gradual transition to a smaller size toward the corners of the mouth.

Besides those of the still living Atlantic Sand shark, the teeth of the now extinct Odontaspis cuspidata (Figure 11) are also to be found along this coast. A larger

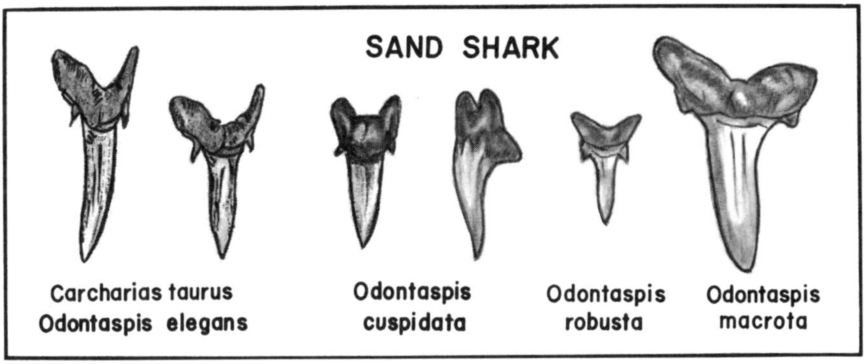

Figure 11.

species than today's Sand shark, it disappeared before the Pleistocene. Its heavier, more robust, awl-shaped teeth are characterized by more pronounced side cusps.

Even less common are the fossil teeth of the Odontaspis robusta and the Odontaspis macrota.

<u>BULL SHARK (Caraharhinus leucas)</u> <u>Figure 12.</u>

Sometimes also called the Cub shark, this member of the requiem shark family (Carcharhinidae) is the only known shark that also frequents fresh water (e.g. Lake Okeechobee, Florida). Running from a gray to gray-brown above to white below, it has a short, broadly rounded snout with a large dorsal fin placed well forward on its body over the pectoral fins. Reported to lengths of 12 feet and weights of 500 pounds, the Bull is most often seen at lengths of less than 8 feet.

Throughout its range, which includes the Gulf of Mexico, it is abundant in shallow waters, particularly around harbors, bays and estuaries. Its feeding is generally correlated with tidal movements. Under some circumstances, it is a vicious shark and has been known to attack bathers and skin divers.

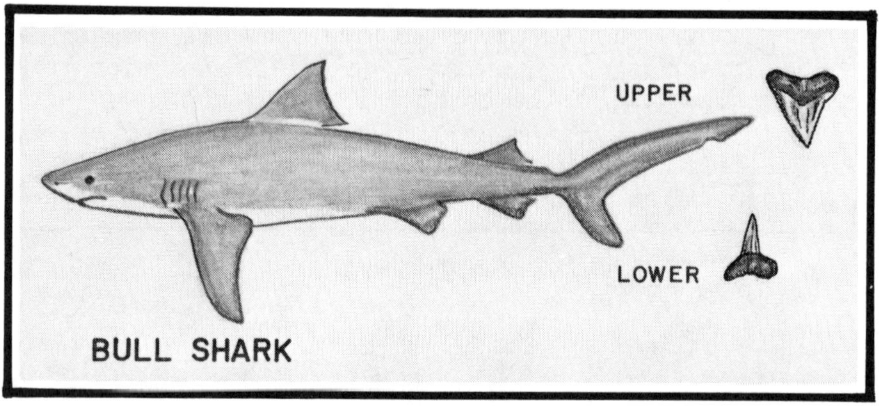

Figure 12.

The Bull shark is one of the species that show markedly different teeth in the upper and lower jaws. The serrated uppers are somewhat triangular, like the cutting teeth of other species, while the lowers tend to be more narrow and fang-like in appearance. Good sized specimens of this shark's teeth are typically not much over 3/4" long.

<u>LEMON SHARK (Negaprion brevirostris)</u> <u>Figure 13.</u>

Another of the requiem shark (Carcharhinidae) family, the Lemon is a fairly common tropical shark readily recognized by its yellowish-brown color. While reaching lengths of about 11 feet, this two-dorsal-finned shark is not as heavy and as bulky as other sharks of similar length. A 9-1/2 foot specimen, for example, weighed a relatively modest 265 pounds. It is another of the shallow-water sharks. The young, in particular, are apt to be found in very shallow areas. Preying on fishes such as mullet, it feeds more at night than during the day. Its western Atlantic range is from northern Brazil to North Carolina and rarely as far north as New Jersey. This species has also been implicated in attacks on humans; its common occurrence in shallow waters makes it potentially dangerous to bathers.

The Lemon's distinctive teeth are symmetrical and erect in the central part of the jaw; they lack cusps along their margins. Besides a long, smooth-edged crown,

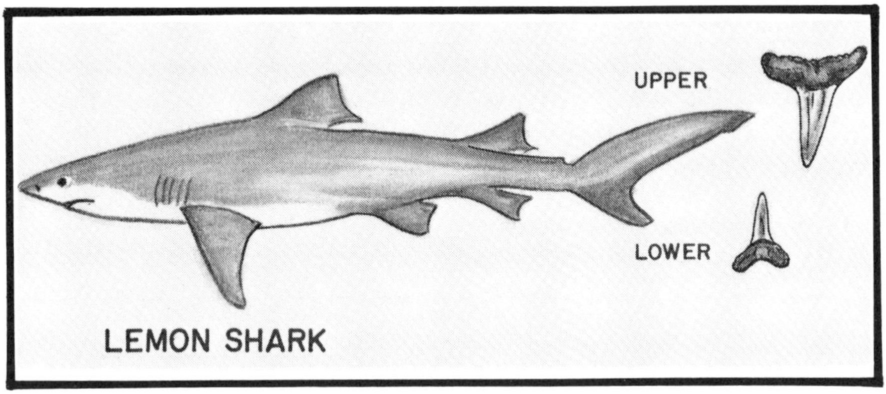

Figure 13.

the base of the upper jaw's teeth has a "wavy," more or less serrated edge. A large fossil tooth of this species runs an inch or more in length.

TIGER SHARK (Galeocerdo cuvieri) Figure 14.

Yet another of the requiem sharks (Carcharhinidae), the Tiger grows to considerably larger sizes than its relatives, the Bull and Lemon. The known maximum length is 18 feet, but reports of 30-foot specimens persist. A Tiger in the 13- to 14-foot range may weigh well over 1000 pounds. A 13 foot, 10-1/2 inch long Tiger taken by rod and reel off a North Carolina pier weighed 1780 pounds. It had a 103 inch girth. Larger fish easily exceed 2000 pounds.

Young Tigers have characteristic bars and spots on their back and upper sides but large adults are usually a plainer, brownish-gray color. This species is also characterized by a short, broadly rounded, sharp-pointed snout with a large front dorsal set relatively far forward on a rather elongated body.

A tropical and sub-tropical species throughout the world, the Tiger is frequently found in coastal waters as well as off-shore. It is most abundant in the Caribbean-south Florida region, seeming to move northward and southward with the seasons. It is known to enter very shallow waters. While a fairly sluggish fish under some conditions, it becomes voracious and a more active, powerful swimmer in the presence of food. Such food includes all forms of living as well as dead matter. In fact, a Tiger will apparently eat almost anything. Besides fishes, squid, crabs and other sharks, it also feeds on turtles and sea lions. A vast assortment of non-digestible items have also been found in its stomach, including cans, bottles, shoes, a sack of coal, dogs and even parts of a crocodile. It is believed to be more active at night than during the day.

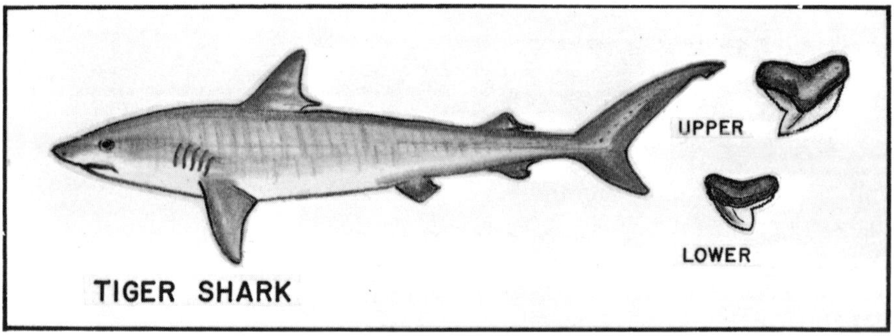

Figure 14.

This shark has been responsible for known attacks on skin divers and bathers. It is among the limited number of sharks classified as man-eaters.

First appearing in the mid-Pliocene, the teeth of the Tiger are unique among sharks. Alike in both the upper and lower jaw, they are recurved, notched at their outer margins, and have coarsely serrated edges. They decrease in size toward the corner of the mouth. They are an efficient, powerful, cutting tool. The tooth is akin to a bread knife and cuts in much the same fashion. In transporting the preserved whole jaws of these fish, some careless handlers have received gashes of almost surgical precision. It has been domonstrated that a man can shave the hair off his forearm with a large tooth from an adult Tiger.

The fossil teeth of the Tiger shark are less common along the Venice beaches than those of the Sand, Bull and Lemon. And, because of their unique configuration, they tend to be not as long as those of several smaller shark species. They are, nevertheless, particularly broad for their size. Most fossils from this species run less than 1" in length.

Also to be found along this section of the Gulf coast are the fossil teeth of an earlier relative of today's Tiger shark, the Galeocerdo adundus (Figure 15). With both the upper and lower teeth of similar configuration, the fossils of this shark - which had disappeared by the mid-Pliocene - are generally straighter crowned and not quite as massive as those of today's Tiger.

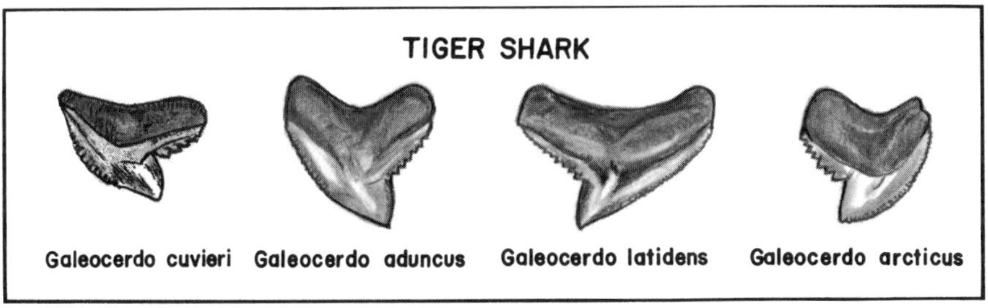

Figure 15.

Other less frequent finds are the fossil teeth of the Galeocerdo latidens and the Galeocerdo arcticus.

DUSKY SHARK (Carcharhinus obscurus) — Figure 16.

The Dusky, another of the requiem sharks, is found in tropical and sub-tropical parts of the Atlantic, with its center of abundance apparently around Florida. Known to grow to lengths of 12 feet and reported as large as 14, the adult tends to be a bluish to leaden-gray above and whitish underneath. There is a darker coloration at the pectoral tips. It has a long, pointed snout. Besides well-developed pectoral fins, it has a high first dorsal which is much larger than the second.

Although sometimes found in shallow waters, the Dusky is most frequently found offshore and well away from shoal waters. It is considered dangerous to man.

The upper and lower teeth of the Dusky differ in somewhat the same manner as those of the Bull shark. The upper teeth are nearly triangular in shape and are serrated; the lower are more slender, have a broad base and are more finely serrated.

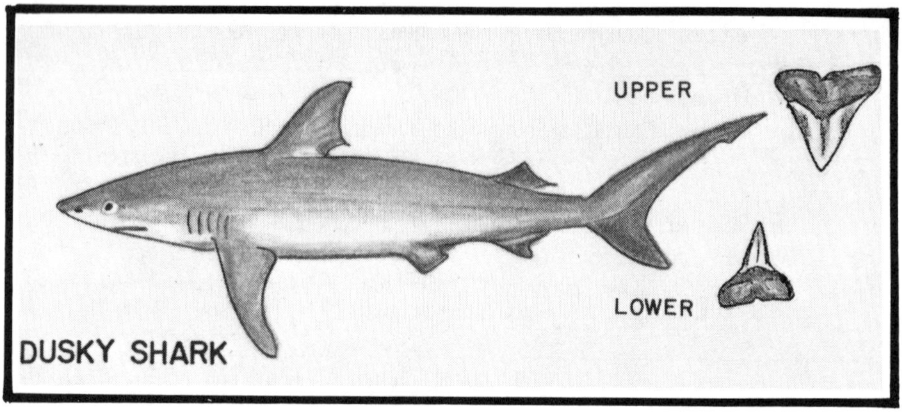

Figure 16.

The teeth of the requiem shark families, Dusky, Bull, Blacktip, Spinner and Brown, are all very similar in appearance. It is extremely difficult, and sometimes impossible, to tell one from another. It takes an expert, who has made an intensive study of sharks, to do so.

BLACKTIP SHARK (Carcharninus limbatus) Figure 17.

Seldom growing to more than 6 feet in length, the Blacktip is an active, strong-swimming tropical water shark which has frequently been seen leaping from the water. Occurring both in-shore and off, it feeds on small fish and rays. A widespread fish, its body ranges from a dark gray to blue-gray or yellowish-gray on top

Figure 17.

to yellowish-white or white underneath. It characteristically has black tips on the pectoral fins (as do several other species of sharks) and a dark band along its side up to about the pelvic region. The dorsal and anal fins and the lower lobe of the caudal fin are also black-tipped. It is not ranked as one of the sharks dangerous to man.

The Blacktip's teeth are similar in the upper and lower jaws. They are regularly serrated from their bases to their tips. As already noted, they are very similar to those of other requiem sharks.

SPINNER SHARK (Carcharhinus maculipimis)

The strong-swimming Spinner, another of the requiem sharks, grows to lengths of 8 feet. Gray above and white below, it has a faint dark band on its sides up to its pelvic fins. It has particularly long gill slits. Like the Blacktip, it has well-marked black tips on its fins. It too is commonly observed leaping from the water and twisting. It is known to frequent very shallow waters and flats. At least one recorded attack on man has been attributed to this shark.

The fossil teeth of this requiem shark are very similar to those of the Bull, Dusky, Blacktip and Brown.

SANDBAR or BROWN SHARK (Carcharhinus milberti)

Somewhat resembling the Bull, this fairly common shark reaches lengths of nearly 8 feet and weights of about 250 pounds. Its general range is from southern Brazil to southern New England. Varying from a gray to brown above to a white below, it is in part identifiable by a high dorsal fin and a lack of fin markings. A shallow-water resident, it feeds largely on bottom-living fish. There have been no recorded attacks by this shark on man.

Its fossil teeth are almost identical to those of the preceding members of the requiem shark family.

GREAT HAMMERHEAD (Sphyrna mokarran) Figure 18.

Easily recognizable by its rather grotesque, hammer-shaped head, this is a large, strong-swimming warm-water shark found in Florida waters as well as elsewhere in the Atlantic and parts of the Pacific oceans. Reaching lengths of 18 feet and more than 1700 pounds in weight, specimens of 13 and 14 feet are relatively common. It is usually a brownish-gray to olive above, paling to a lighter color beneath. Because of its size, it is considered to be dangerous to man. Even the smaller fish are often aggressive. Attacks on man have been recorded but it is not certain whether they were made by the Great Hammerhead or related species, such as the Scalloped Hammerhead or Smooth Hammerhead. The Smooth Hammerhead (Sphyrna zygaena) has a higher more erect dorsal than the Sphyrna mokarran. While reaching lengths of 13 feet and weights of at least 900 pounds, it is still smaller than the up to 1700 pound Great Hammerhead.

Figure 18.

Yet another member of this family, the Scalloped Hammerhead (Sphyrna lewini), is known to reach lengths of 10 feet. It is distinguished from the other members of this species by variations in the shape of its head and fins.

The teeth of the Great Hammerhead are serrated, while those of the Scalloped and Smooth species are not. Comparatively small, they are similar in the upper and lower jaws. They are notched and, with the exception of a few central teeth, directed toward the sides.

Hammerheads are believed to prey a great deal on rays. One large shark brought into Florida's Mote Marine Laboratory had 96 sting ray barbs imbedded in and about its mouth, jaws and head.

MAKO SHARK (Isurus oxyrinchus) Figure 19.

An open-ocean shark of the mackerel (lamnidae) family, a Mako over 12 feet long and weighing 1,061 pounds was taken by rod and reel in 1970 off New Zealand. An even larger 1,175 pound specimen was harpooned in Atlantic Ocean waters off Rhode Island. Somewhat resembling the dreaded man-eating Great White shark, the Mako has the same streamlined shape and nearly symmetrical tail. Characterized by a pointed snout, its color ranges from a brilliant cobalt to bluish-gray on top to white beneath.

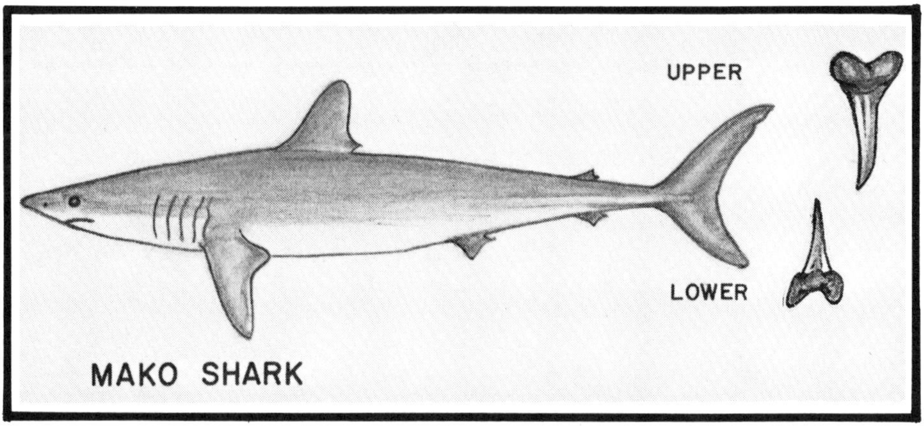

Figure 19.

In dead specimens, however, the color fades to a grayish-brown on top. Occurring in tropical and warmer parts of the Atlantic, the fast-swimming Mako - sometimes called the Blue Pointer - is almost entirely a "blue water" fish. Although seen in Bahama waters of only about 30 feet in depth, it is characteristically found much further out, where it apparently swims near the surface to feed on smaller fish such as mackeral and tuna. In fact, these fish are often seen swimming with the tips of the first dorsal fin and tail above the surface.

Actually protruding from its mouth, the teeth of the Mako are long and slender. There is little difference between those in the upper and lower jaw. In comparison to the somewhat similar teeth of the Sand shark, those of the modern day Mako are generally broader and more massive. They are inward-curving without secondary cusps and without serrations along the edges. There are usually two central teeth in the front of the jaw that are more slender than the others.

Besides the still-living Mako species, the teeth of its extinct predessor, the Isurus hastalis, are also to be found among the Gulf coast fossils (Figure 20). While

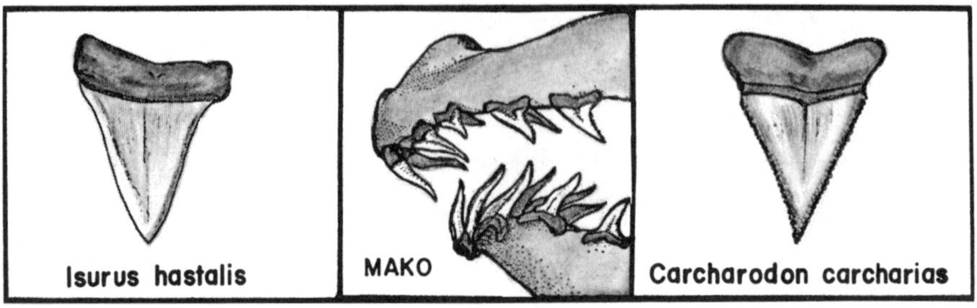

Figure 20.

not available in large numbers, these teeth are not uncommon. Much broader than those of the extant Mako, they do not have a serrated edge such as the large teeth of the Great White shark. While larger ones may occur, a 2" long Isurus hastalis fossil tooth is a good-sized specimen.

GREAT WHITE SHARK (Carcharodon carcharias) Figure 21.

Also known as Man-eater, White Death and White Pointer, the Great White is undoubtedly the most fearsome, well-armed and deadliest of the living sharks inhabiting today's seas. They are incredibly aggressive, savage almost beyond belief! It was a monstrous, terrorizing 25 footer of this species that was popularized in the exciting book and movie "Jaws."

Although a 36-1/2 foot shark was reportedly taken in 1936, subsequent studies of other captured specimens of up to 21 feet in length have raised serious doubts about the authenticity of this record. Tooth and jaw dimensions of substantially smaller fish have exceeded those of this supposedly 36-1/2 foot shark. From comparative tooth measurements, it is believed the length of this fish was erroneously recorded as 36-1/2 feet when it should have been 16-1/2. If this is so, then the largest known Great White shark is a 21-foot fish taken off of

Cuba. It reportedly weighed 7,300 pounds. Bite measurements on whale carcasses also suggest Great Whites of 25 to 27 feet in length were responsible for such monstrous imprints. A 17-1/2 foot, 3,100-pound shark was harpooned off the California coast in late 1975. An equally as long but heavier fish was harpooned off Montauk Point in June, 1964. It had a girth of 13 feet and weighed 4,500 pounds.

From fish such as these and other observations, it is believed Great Whites of as much as 30 feet in length may be cruising the seas even today.

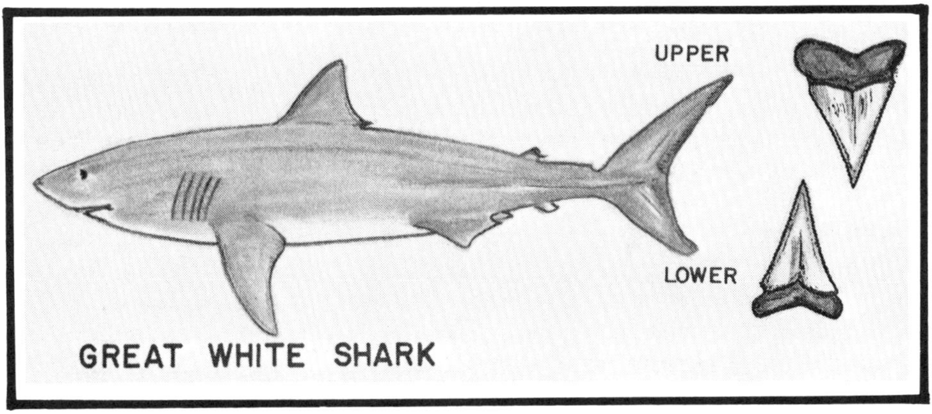

Figure 21.

With a pointed snout, a streamlined form, and a crescent-shaped, nearly equal lobed caudal fin, the Great White has a much deeper, heavier body than its relative, the Mako. Its color is grayish-brown, slate-blue or gray on top, fading to a dirty white below. Very large sharks are a more leaden-white. There is usually a black spot near the base of the pectoral fins. Fortunately, it is a "blue water" fish, generally roaming the tropic and more temperate waters of the sea. At no place is it considered a common specie. It feeds on other sharks, sea turtles, sea lions, seals and other large creatures, which may help explain its attack on divers. Whole sea lions have been found in its stomach, as have been the remains of other sharks from 4 to 7 feet long. It also scavenges on dead flesh and refuse. It is a fearless, voracious, agile, strong fish that has been described by some as the world's most ferocious animal.

The Great White is considered an extremely dangerous

fish to swimmers and divers. Besides being implicated in several attacks on divers in off-shore waters, it is known to skirt shorelines occasionally in search of food. When this occurs in a populated area, it is apt to attack swimmers. From the teeth later dug out of their hulls, this shark has been identified in several known attacks on boats. In fact, it is believed Great Whites will attack just about anything.

When hooked or harpooned, the Great White remains a dangerous adversary. Veteran anglers say it is possibly the swiftest and most agile of all the sharks. The fact that Great Whites regularly catch and eat seals is ample testimony to their speed.

The large teeth of the Great White are triangular in shape with coarsely serrated edges (Figure 22). Similar in both jaws, they are cutting teeth. Because of the relative rarity of these sharks, their teeth are not regularly found among the Venice beach fossils. When found, a 2" long tooth would be an unusually long one. The teeth, however, of this shark's now extinct, even larger predecessor, the huge Carcharodon megalodon, are found with surprising regularity. They are often substantially larger than any taken from today's Great White

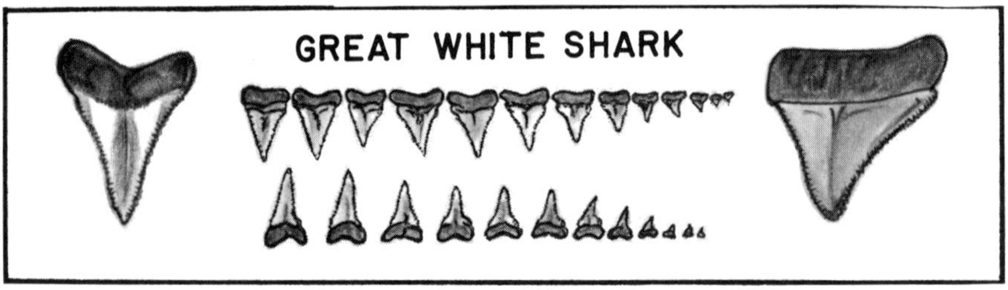

Figure 22.

shark. So are those of two other less common but related species, the Carcharodon auriculatus and the Carcharodon sulcidens.

CARCHARODON MEGALODON Figure 23.

These giant predecessors to the fierce, aggressive Great White shark are believed to have first appeared in the Miocene epoch. They probably became extinct in relatively recent times, perhaps 10,000 to 50,000 years ago. In many respects, these huge carnivores retained features of their ancestors, Carcharodon praemegalodon weiler of Oligocene times.

Based on the enormous size of their fossil teeth, these fish have been estimated to grow from a very conservative 50 feet to what some believe to have been over 100 feet in length. They may have even exceeded the size of the Blue whale, a creature known to reach 113 feet in length and an estimated 170 tons in weight. Most paleontologists, however, think these fish reached lengths more like 70 to 80 feet. They undoubtedly rank as the largest carnivores to have lived on earth.

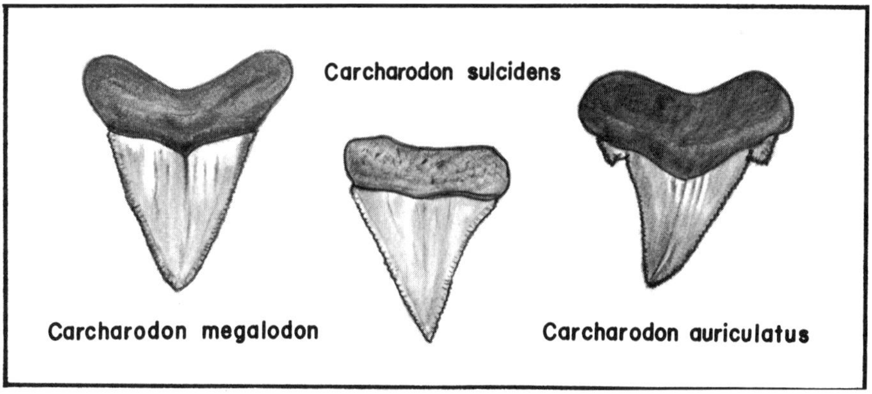

Figure 23.

The bearer of teeth up to 8" in overall length, these monstrous, wide-ranging predators were well-armed for their environmental niche in the Tertiary seas. While large numbers have been found along both coasts of the United States as well as on the ocean bottom up to several hundred miles off-shore, their fossil teeth are probably no more plentiful in any one locale than around Venice, Florida. Much sought-after by shark tooth hunters, the Carcharodon megalodon teeth are prized by both amateur and professional collectors alike. Specimens of 4" and more in slant height are not unusual. Similar in shape and structure to those of today's fearsome Great White, the teeth of this extinct member of the Mackerel shark family (lammidae) are triangular in shape with serrated cutting edges. On well-preserved specimens, these serrations are clearly in evidence. Sometimes as large as a man's hand, they are thick, solid, massive teeth.

Like the sharks of today, all these great fish also had cartilaginous skeletons. Consequently, when they died, the entire carcass decomposed relatively quickly. So, aside from their huge teeth, there is no way of knowing for certain just how large they really were. It still remains a matter of scientific speculation. The best estimates of their probable dimensions are undoubtedly those derived from measurements taken on large, captured Great White sharks. Tooth and jaw size have been related to each fish's weight and length. From these data, a projection has been made predicting fish size based on the enamel length of the largest tooth taken from the shark's upper jaw. This prediction assumes the Carcharodon megalodon was very similar in size and appearance to today's Great White. As shown in Figure 24, the enamel height of the largest upper tooth in a 50-

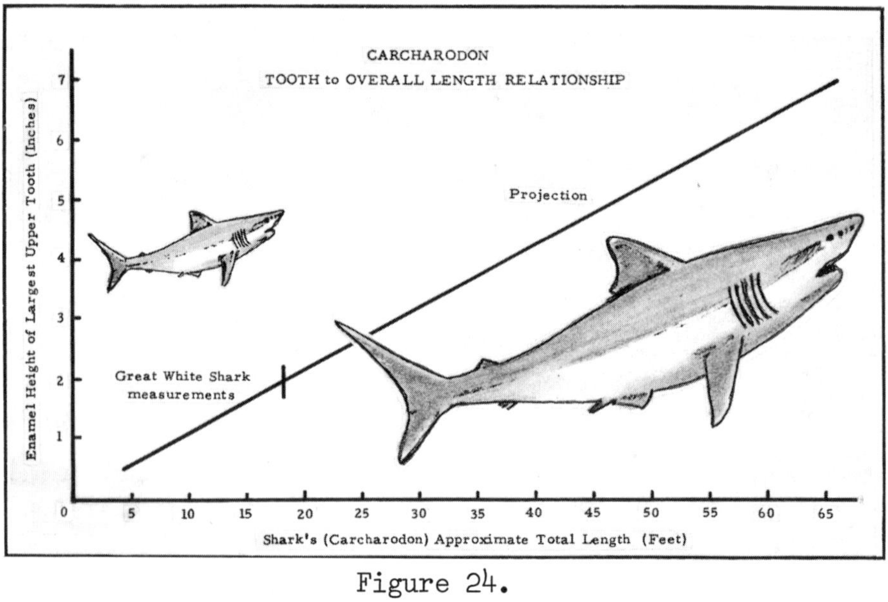

Figure 24.

foot-long shark is projected to be 5-1/4". When an individual fossil tooth specimen is found, it is difficult enough to tell with certainty whether it came from the upper or lower jaw, much less whether it was the largest. In all probability, it is one of the several dozen smaller functional teeth or from one of the back-up rows. So, if the measurements of a tooth from an unknown location in the fish's jaw is used to estimate its overall size, the results will probably understate the deceased shark's size.

Although there is little tangible evidence of just how aggressive and fearless these box-car-sized sharks were, all indications are that there was nothing in the seas they feared or couldn't out-swim. Their broken-off teeth have been found embedded in the fossil vertebrates of whales upon which they apparently fed. Their dagger-tooth jaws are believed to have opened a gaping 6 feet or more, room for most men to walk through without even stooping over. Shown on the cover of this book is the reconstruction of such a jaw at New York's American Museum of Natural History. With mouths of this size, these fish had the capacity to gulp down full-sized porpoises or walrus in a single bite.

Why did these awesome creatures vanish from the seas of the world? There is no positive answer to this. Some speculate that the Ice Age may have been a factor. But with their mobility, it is unlikely that it was simply a matter of colder temperatures. It is also questionable that their food supply was reduced to such a large degree. Instead, why they dropped from sight is yet another of the unsolved mysteries of the past. But, some ask, are they actually extinct? Some researchers and marine life investigators think these enormous sharks may still inhabit our seas even today. Consider, if you will, the following:

-In 1918, Dr. David G. Stead of Sydney, Australia reported the sighting of an immense shark of almost unbelievable proportions near Port Stephens on the

New South Wales coast. It caused such a fright that the deep water cray fishermen refused to go to sea for several days after the event. Eye witnesses, men of the sea and used to its environment, estimated the length of the shark to have been at least 115 feet long to as much as 300. Yes, 300 feet! While considered absurd by most, this is what members of the crew reported. The huge, ghostly white fish appeared at the fishing grounds devouring one crayfish pot after another. These roughly 3 foot 6 inch diameter pots often hold as many as two to three dozen good-sized crayfish. The seasoned seamen said it was definitely not a whale. The head, they reported, was "at least as large as the roof of the wharf shed at Nelson's Bay." It was larger than any living creature they had ever seen.

-Giant, 5-inch across-the-base shark's teeth have been dredged up from deep, central Pacific waters. While their size alone was unusual, that was not the only impressive thing about them. They weren't fossilized! They were of relatively recent origin.

-In Atlantic Ocean waters near the mysterious Bermuda "Triangle," one of the new breed of underwater exploratory vehicles registered a totally unexpected sonar reading on a relatively fast moving underwater object estimated to be as much as 100 feet in length. Surface crafts in that same part of the sea reported no whale sightings that day. Not only were no Navy submarines reportedly in the area, the unidentified object was traveling at a speed in excess of any known man-made submersible. At the time, it was thought to have some unexplained relationship to the ship and airplane disappearances in the "Triangle." But could it have been one of these giant sharks?

-In the 1960's along the outer edge of Australia's Great Barrier Reef, an 85 foot ship experienced engine trouble which forced it to weigh anchor for repairs. Although the men subsequently refused to openly report what they had seen for fear of public ridicule, the captain and his crew later told friends of sighting an immense shark as it moved slowly past their ship. Whitish in color, they were awed by its size. It was as long if not longer than their boat! Experienced men of the sea, they too were certain the creature was not a whale.

Could it be that the Carcharodon megalodon is not extinct, that a few of these huge predators still live? Tentacle scars found on deep-diving whales attest to the size of unseen, monstrous squids that apparently live in the unexplored depths of our seas. They might be one potential food source for any deep-water living whale-size shark.

For those who say it is absurd to even think such a huge creature could live in today's sea undetected by man, consider if you will a recent chance happening in Pacific Ocean waters. In November, 1976, off Oahu in the Hawaiian Islands, the carcass of a previously unheard of species of shark was found accidentally entangled in a Navy vessel's anchor line. It was twelve-feet long and weighed an estimated 1,500 pounds. Entrapped some place between the 500 and 1,000 foot level, the huge creature apparently suffocated when its forward motion was stopped and it could no longer flow enough water over its gills.

CARCHARODON AURICULATUS and CARCHARODON SULCIDENS

The teeth of these two now extinct relatives of today's Great White shark are also apt to be among the fossils found by collectors. They, however, occur far less frequently than those of the larger C. megalodon.

The teeth of the C. auriculatus generally have lateral denticles which are uncommon on the C. megalodon. Both the blade of the tooth and the side cusps are serrated. This shark's upper teeth are triangular in shape while the lowers are narrower, deeper and tend toward a longer central cusp. Large specimens run 2" to 3" in length.

Similar in size to those of the C. auriculatus, the C. sulcidens' teeth somewhat resemble those of the Great White shark. They, however, are nearly straight across at the root base whereas those of the Great White are curved toward the tooth's tip. Both have serrated edges. While sometimes confused with the teeth of the extinct Mako shark, the Isurus hastalis, the edge serrations clearly identify the C. sulcidens. Those of the Isurus hastalis are smooth-edged.

HEMIPRISTIS SERRA and Others   Figure 25.

This shark, which is another of the now extinct species in this part of the world, was common in the seas of the early Tertiary period. Also a member of the requiem shark family, its teeth have coarse edge serrations like those of the Carcharodon megalodon. Fossil tooth specimens of over 1" in length are not unusual.

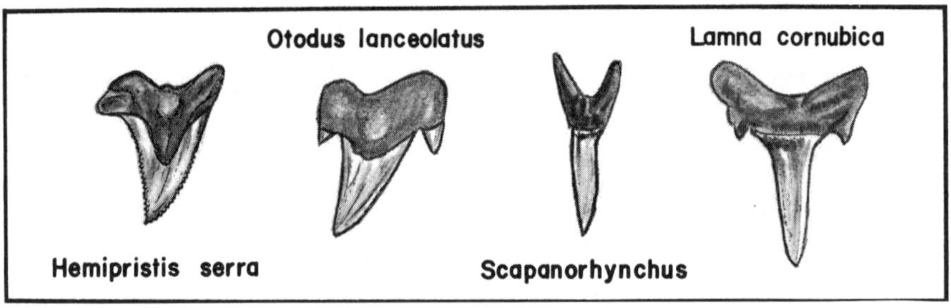

Figure 25.

Also shown in Figure 25 are three other but far less commonly found tooth specimens.

BLUE SHARK (Prionace glauca)   Figure 26.

One of the most common of the oceanic sharks, the Blue is found throughout the temperate and tropical waters of the world. A slender, beautifully colored shark, it runs from a bright cobalt coloration on its back to a snowy-white underneath. Also known as the Blue Whaler, it has particularly long pectoral fins. This shark is reported to reach lengths of 20 feet. While usually found well off-shore, they do occasionally come inshore and into shallow waters. Generally a near-the-surface feeder, Blues have been implicated in attacks on swimmers. They are also believed to have been responsible for attacks on military personnel in several war-time tragedies.

While their teeth are not long by shark standards, they are large and particularly sharp. Blues have been observed effortlessly ripping 20-pound bites off whale carcasses. The teeth are unlike in the two jaws; the uppers are sub-triangular in outline and have serrated edges; the lowers are narrower, more erect and also serrated.

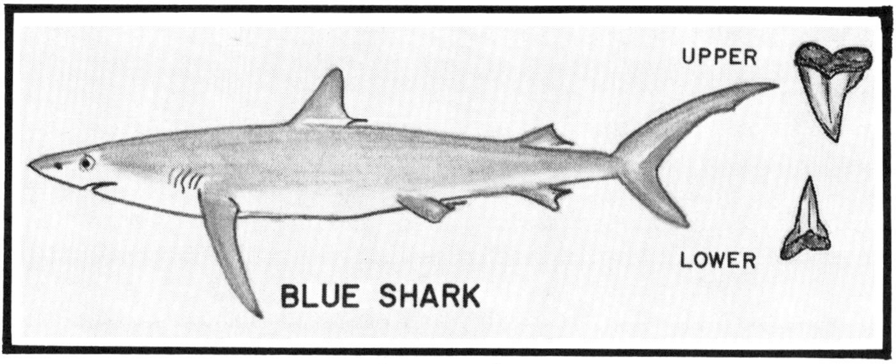

Figure 26.

THRESHER SHARK (*Alopias vulpinus*) Figure 27.

Easily recognizable by its tail, which is about as long as its body, the Thresher occurs almost entirely in the open seas. Growing to lengths of 20 feet and weights of as much as 1,000 pounds, this species is found at or near the surface in the cooler ocean waters. In the eastern Atlantic, it occurs from the Gulf of St. Lawrence to northern Argentina. It is most frequently

Figure 27.

sighted off southern New England. Using its long tail to herd and stun its prey, this shark feeds almost entirely on schooling fish. There are no indications it is dangerous to man.

The teeth of the Thresher are relatively small for a fish of its size.

WHITETIP SHARK (Carcharhinus longimanus) Figure 28.

Reaching lengths of 13 feet, the Whitetip is almost entirely a pelagic species occurring far out at sea. It is practically never found in waters less than 100 fathoms deep. It is extraordinarily abundant and, according to some authoritative sources, may possibly be "the most abundant large animal - large being over 100 pounds- on the face of the Earth." In most specimens, the pectoral, pelvic and first dorsal fins and the lobes of the caudal fin are light or white-tipped in the adult. The shark itself ranges in color from light gray, pale brown

Figure 28.

or slate-blue on top to a yellowish-brown to dull-white underneath. Whitetips are considered a serious threat to open-water divers.

WHALE SHARK (Rhincodon typus) Figure 29.

This plankton- and small sea-life feeder is the largest of the modern day sharks. It is a docile, slow, lumbering creature. Reaching lengths of 60 feet or more, a captured 38-foot specimen weighed an estimated 26,600 pounds. An off-shore fish, it is found in the tropical waters of all oceans. Its back and sides are a red or greenish-brown to dark gray and covered with scattered white or yellow spots. It also shows some transverse white or yellow stripes. Its lower body is a whitish to yellowish color.

Not considered dangerous to man, this giant fish relies

upon its large mouth and numerous minute teeth to filter small prey from the sea waters. Its teeth, in fact, are probably the most numerous of all the sharks - close to 7200. But they are also among the very smallest, running only an eighth-of-an-inch in height. Little,

Figure 29.

however, is known of its life history.

PORBEAGLE (Lamna nasus) Figure 30.

Also known as the Mackerel Shark, the Porbeagle is a fast-swimming, heavy-bodied, open-ocean fish closely resembling its family relatives, the Mako and Great White. Differing from these other two, however, is the location of the Porbeagle's second dorsal, which is located directly above its anal fin. Its caudal fin is also less symmetrical than that of the White or Mako, the upper lobe being decidedly longer. Ranging from a dark blue-gray to blackish on top, its color becomes white on the lower sides and under-surface. While most are 4 to 5 feet long, the largest reported specimens approach lengths of 13 feet. A captured 9-footer weighed 400 pounds.

Generally found in near-shore waters off the east coast of North America from the Newfoundland Banks to South Carolina, it is most common north of Cape Cod. Feeding to a large extent on herring and mackerel, it ranges from the sea's surface downward to at least 480 feet.

The Porbeagle's teeth somewhat resemble those of the Mako, except that they usually have pronounced secondary cusps on each side of the main cusp.

Figure 30.

NURSE SHARK (Ginglymostoma cirratun) Figure 31.

A widespread, shallow water fish, the Nurse shark has a gray-brown to yellow-brown upper body with the remainder of its body tending toward lighter shades of these same colors. It has two almost equal size, relatively close together dorsal fins and long barbels in front of each nostril. Behind its blunt, rounded snout, its eyes are unusually small. Its mouth and many cusped teeth are small for a shark. On the other hand, its fins are comparatively large and its tail particularly long.

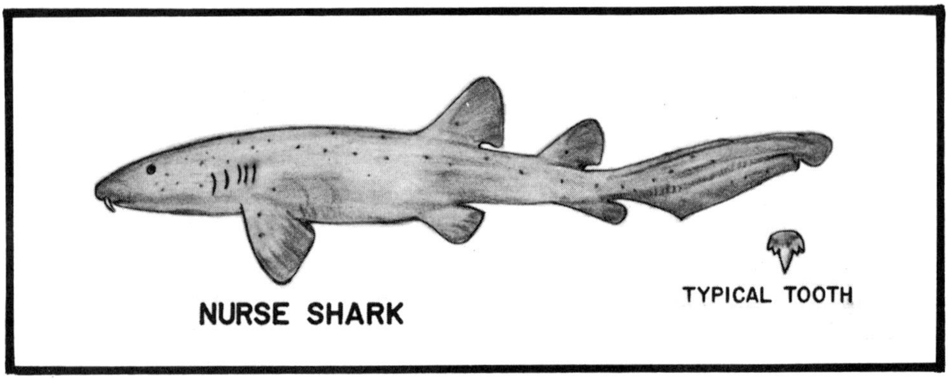

Figure 31.

A relatively sluggish fish, the Nurse is often found resting in shallow underwater caves or under protective ledges. It is chiefly found inshore, often in water less than 10 feet deep. While not considered dangerous to man, it can be when harassed or otherwise provoked. Despite its relatively feeble teeth, it is capable of inflicting painful bites.

The Nurse reaches lengths of up to 14 feet but is not a heavy-bodied fish. A captured 8-1/2 foot specimen, for example, weighed 350 pounds. The Nurse is most common in southern Florida and Caribbean waters, seldom being found above North Carolina.

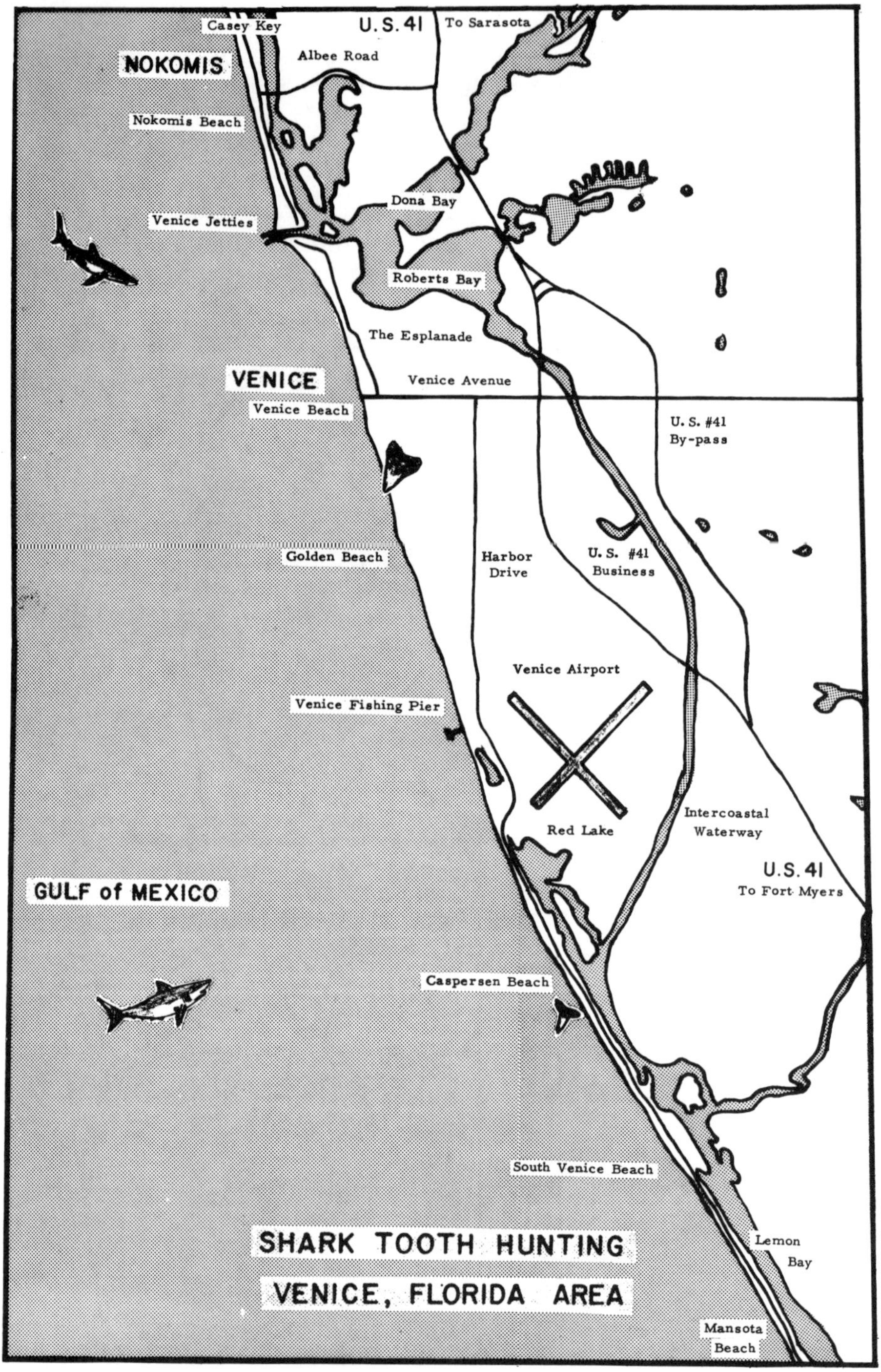
Casey Key
U.S. 41
To Sarasota
NOKOMIS
Albee Road
Nokomis Beach
Dona Bay
Venice Jetties
Roberts Bay
The Esplanade
VENICE
Venice Avenue
Venice Beach
U. S. #41
By-pass
Golden Beach
Harbor
Drive
U. S. #41
Business
Venice Airport
Venice Fishing Pier
Red Lake
Intercoastal
Waterway
U.S. 41
To Fort Myers
GULF of MEXICO
Caspersen Beach
South Venice Beach
SHARK TOOTH HUNTING
VENICE, FLORIDA AREA
Lemon
Bay
Mansota
Beach

Figure 32.

HUNTING METHODS AND SITES

Knowing what the different sharks' teeth look like is one thing; finding them is another. Besides being able to determine what are and aren't productive areas in which to hunt, the tooth hunter should also know how to assess other factors which can affect his chances of success. Along the sea coast, tides and weather conditions play a significant role. Inland, soil and surface configurations warrant close attention. And whether inland or at coastal sites, the tooth hunter should be aware of a few simple tools and mechanical aids that can be of tremendous assistance in separating fossil teeth from the dirt and sand in which they are found.

While beach hunting is probably the most popular and appealing of the fossil tooth collecting methods, excellent finds are also made at various inland sites and in the shallow off-shore coastal waters.

Beach Sites

One of the most productive fossil shark tooth collecting beaches in the United States is along the Gulf coast at Venice, Florida (Figure 32). Year after year, large quantities of gracefully-formed, jewelry-grade specimens are collected from these shores. In addition to those of the more plentiful Bull, Lemon, Sand and Tiger sharks, a sizeable number of two-inch and longer Carcharodon megalodon teeth are also recovered. They are found scattered over many miles of this coast line. Besides the more isolated coastal stretches such as Caspersen Beach, teeth are also regularly found in the surf directly in front of many of the ocean front condominiums. In fact, a sizeable number are found nearly every day of the week on the tidal flats and in the shell piles right on the Venice Avenue Public Beach. It is not at all unusual for a tooth hunter to walk less than 100 feet from his parked car and begin picking up fossil teeth.

While found in great abundance throughout the world, fossil shark teeth are found in particularly large numbers at Venice, Florida. Yet there are numerous other places both in Florida and elsewhere in the United States that also consistently provide attractive specimens. Some excellent finds, for example, are made along parts of the Maryland, New Jersey and North Carolina shorelines. Chesapeake Bay's Calvert and Scientist Cliffs are well known hunting grounds as is Sharktooth Hill near Bakersfield, California. Numerous deposits in Nebraska, Iowa and Illinois have produced display-quality specimens. So have the banks of many of the rivers emptying into the Atlantic and into the Gulf of Mexico. Mississippi's Tombigbee River, for example, is one such place.

For beach and coastal sites, any place where there are sedimentary rocks along the shore and a gently sloping sea bottom is apt to be a good fossil collecting area. Fossil bearing deposits may be part of the offshore sea bottom or part of the land exposed to the sea along the coast line. It is from such rocks that entrapped fossils are freed by the forces of nature.

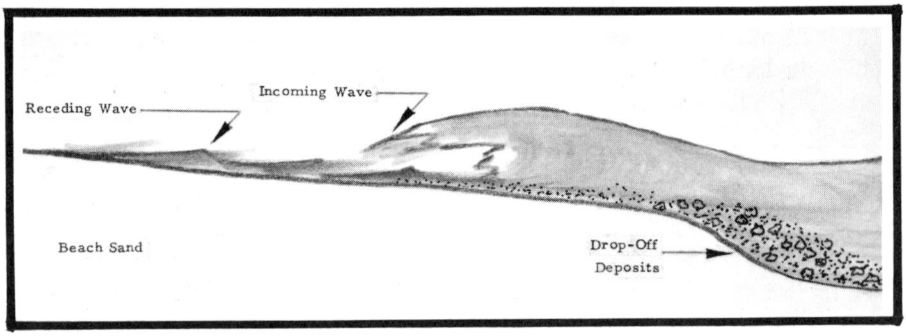

Figure 33.

In looking for a fossil bearing section of shoreline, the color of the beach sand is an important indicator. Generally, fossils - including sharks' teeth - are found in far greater abundance where there is dark, blackish-colored, fossiliferous sand. At Venice, for example, long stretches of the beach are of this color and texture. On such beaches, tooth hunters look for areas where the natural action of the water tends to pile up shell fragments, small rocks, and similar-sized objects. They particularly look for dark brown and black shattered bits of fossil bone. Such bones are usually distinguishable from ordinary rocks by the multitude of tiny holes and channels in them. This is where the animal's blood vessels, nerves and other tissues once ran. Experienced shark tooth hunters know that they will invariably score best when they find deposits rich in such fossils and fossil fragments.

Along a fossiliferous beach, a particularly favorable collecting situation that veteran tooth hunters look for is what they call a "wash-in". To better understand just what a "wash-in" is and how it occurs requires consideration of the near-shore sea bottom itself. Figure 33 shows what this gently sloping surface typically looks like along the Gulf adjacent to Venice, Florida. Where the surf sweeps back into the sea, there is usually a small but sharp six-inch to over one foot drop-off in the sea bottom. It is a point of exceptionally high water turbulence. Along this shore-paralleling trough, there is often a heavy accumulation of pebbles, shells, fossil fragments and other similar objects. While the surf has enough force to carry the lighter grains of sand shoreward, it is not always strong enough to move these heavier particles. Since fossilized sharks' teeth tend to be difficlut to move, they are prone to accumulate in these same off-shore deposits.

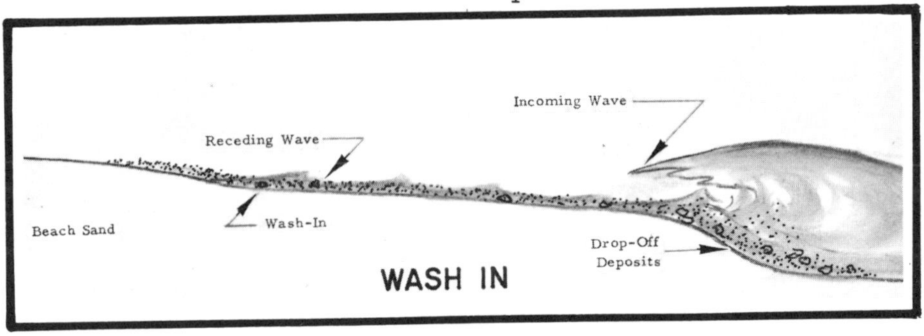

Figure 34.

When the tide routinely changes from low to rising, the strong shoreward surging waves may catch some of this drop-off material and push it up and onto the tidal flats. This is the start of a favorable "wash-in" (Figure 34). Often this material is continuously buffeted back and forth by the incoming and receding waves. A fossil tooth may be swept up onto the sand by one wave, then moments later swept back to sea by the next.

Figure 35 shows two tooth hunters working a favorable "wash-in". Here the beach is littered with an assortment of shells, fossil fragments and other material thrown up by the surf. It is a highly favorable situation for finding fossilized teeth. The teeth don't have to be dug out of the sand; they are to be found randomly mixed in with the other "wash-in" material on top of the tidal flat. Typically some are out in the open where they can be easily picked up, while others are intermixed with the many look-alike bits of shells and fossil chips. It is not unusual, however, to find a great many fossil teeth concentrated in just a very small patch of this material. Experienced tooth hunters often get the best

Figure 35.

results by hunting along the edges of such "wash-ins". Here the bits and pieces are more spread out, making it easier to distinguish any included fossil teeth. As each new wave sweeps up onto the beach then recedes back to sea, much of the "wash-in" material is tumbled about, constantly exposing previously buried particles. Some tooth hunters pick what they believe to be a particularly favorable part along such a "wash-in", then concentrate most of their time and effort on just that one spot. The moving waters and shifting deposits constantly churn new material into view; fossil sharks' teeth are apt to be included.

Usually "wash-ins" do not occur simultaneously over the entire length of a beach. Instead, they may happen over relatively short stretches. Where they do occur, however, tooth hunters should devote a good part of their hunting effort to such places. Understandably, some veteran tooth collectors only hunt on incoming tides when such "wash-ins" are apt to occur.

Another tidal condition favored by many fossil tooth hunters is low tide. When the sea is calm and the water clear, the near-shore drop-off accumulations of shells, rocks, fossils and fossil fragments are under relatively shallow water. In this situation, it is possible to wade along this shore-paralleling trough looking for teeth. Because the smaller sharks' teeth, such as those of the Bull and Lemon, are usually concealed by the larger rocks and shell fragments, this search technique is more applicable to Carcharodon megalodon collecting.

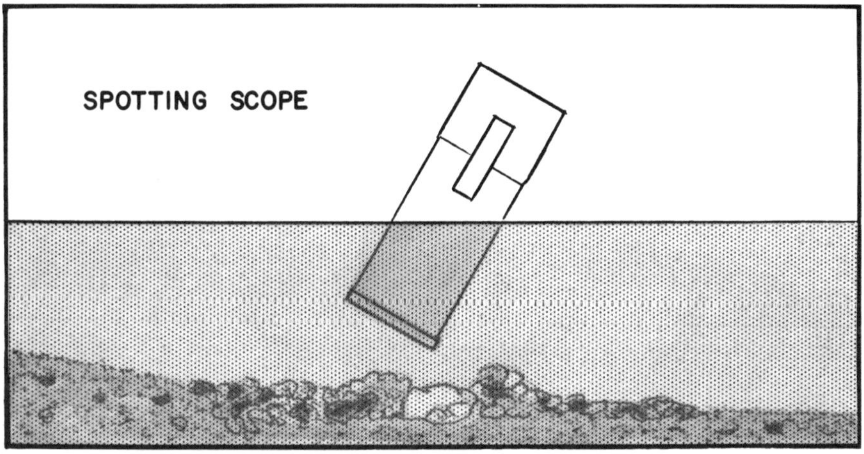

Figure 36.

In this wade-and-search method, it is preferable to work along the shore with the sun to your back. A good pair of polarized sunglasses also helps to reduce the water's surface glare and substantially improve your chances of seeing a fossil tooth that might be lying on the sea bottom. Even so, it is still difficult to distinguish a fossil tooth from an ordinary rock under just a few inches of moving tidal water. A much clearer view can be obtained with a spotting scope (Figure 36). In principle like the view from a glass-bottomed boat, the box has a sealed window at one end and is open at the other. The window end is held under water thus eliminating any surface glare. A much better view of the bottom is obtained in this manner.

While many tooth hunters only work the beaches during low or incoming tides, there are occasions when a high tide can also provide exceptionally good hunting. This is particularly true when a "wash-out" occurs (Figure 37). In this situation, the high, shoreward-driving tidal waters sharply erode or cut away parts of the beach. In so doing, they expose previously buried beds

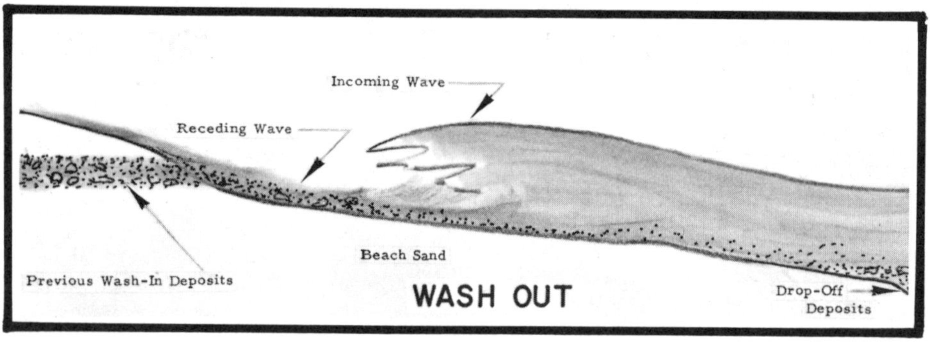

Figure 37.

of shells, fossil chips and small rocks. These beds are very apt to include sharks' teeth. Generally these deposits are the buried remains of earlier "wash-ins", such as those left behind by a storm. The beds of shells and other heavier objects are first washed up on shore by the stormy sea, then subsequently buried by the shifting beach sands. When a "wash-out" occurs, the eroding waves of the high surf cut into these deposits, washing them back toward the sea. As they are pulled seaward, fossil teeth are often briefly exposed on the intervening tidal flat before they are reclaimed by the sea. Tooth hunters often have exceptionally good hunting in such a situation.

Besides favorable tidal washes, a number of other shore line conditions are particularly attractive for tooth hunting. Among these are crevices and channels around sea walls, rock piles and coral formations, as well as creek channels that empty into the sea. At such places, the water running back toward the ocean tends to be channeled into a swifter than normal flow which scours away the lighter beach sands. Often any buried, heavier objects are exposed, including sharks' teeth. Experienced hunters look in places where the seaward-returning tidal currents have cut such deeper than usual channels.

In addition to tidal conditions, the time of day is another consideration in tooth hunting. Many avid tooth hunters - with good reason - favor the very early morning hours. They are on the beach at daybreak. Some, in fact, are on the beach so early they require flashlights to light their way. Yes, flashlights! But there is good reason for them to favor this time. They get first crack at what the sea might have washed in overnight. Since many people prowl the beaches during the daylight hours, any attractive specimens that are washed up on the beach at such times are very apt to be quickly found. But any similar "wash-in" at night will go undetected until the next morning, so the first on the beach get to sort through the overnight tidal deposits.

While "wash-ins", low tides and early morning searches are all applicable to normal day-to-day sea and weather conditions, most hunters agree that one particular set of infrequent hunting circumstances is the best of all: during or after a severe storm. Some of the very best fossil finds occur at these times. Particularly favorable is a strong on-shore wind accompanied by high, incoming seas. Such violent forces invariably tumble all types of sea bottom material shoreward, ultimately hurling many of them up and onto the beach. It may, however, be a day or two after the more violent weather before they start to wash up onto the shore. The sea's power during storms is sometimes awesome. Live shell fish, crabs, even small fish are apt to be thrown up on the shore, as well as great masses of sea weed, chunks of coral, rocks and a vast assortment of shells. Along the fossil bearing shorelines, prehistoric animal bones are very likely to be found among the residue left by the raging seas. So are fossil sharks' teeth, particularly those of the extinct Carcharodon megalodon.

When a storm occurs, serious tooth hunters hit the beach as soon as the subsiding bad weather will permit. It's a time few want to miss. For instance, after Hurricane Agnes in 1973, tooth hunters had a field day along the Venice shore line. A particularly large number of huge Carcharodon megalodon were found, including a sizeable number taken from the storm-piled debris on the Venice Avenue Public Beach.

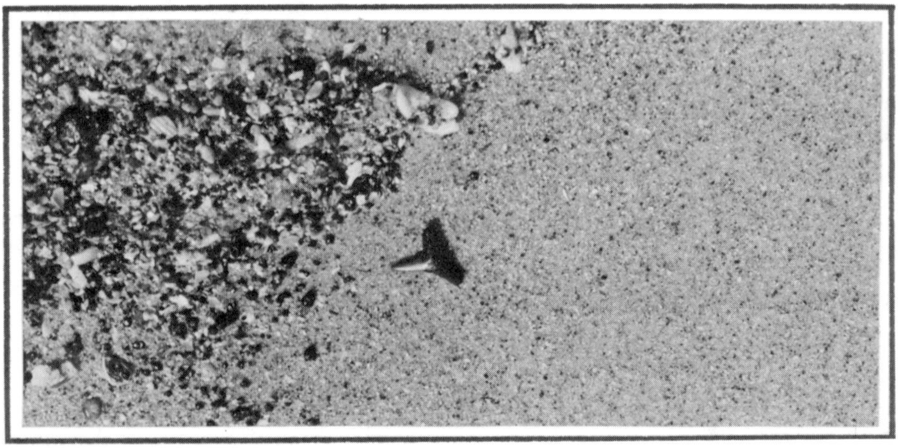

Figure 38.

While knowing when and where to look for fossil teeth on the beach is extremely important, the successful tooth hunter must also be able to distinguish fossil teeth from the look-alike rocks and shells that are scattered along the beach (Figure 38). Some people seem to have a born knack for this; others don't. For one thing, it takes concentration. Instead of broad-brushing a large area, the tooth hunter generally has to focus his attention on just a small patch. He then has to scan every individual rock, shell and fossil fragment to pick out any included teeth. Shape, of course, is one key identifying feature. To a lesser extent, so is color. While the "base" of fossil teeth tend to look like other fossil fragments, the dull, ivory-gray of the tooth's enamel is generally unique among other objects on the beach. With practice and the successful recovery of a few teeth, most beginners quickly acquire the skill of recognizing these fossils. In some situations, prompt recognition is a must. During a "wash-in", for example, an incoming wave is apt to fan out an array of fossil-bearing deposits on the tidal flats as it recedes. Fossil teeth are likely to be scattered among the pieces strewn across the beach. The tooth hunter has just a few seconds to recognize a tooth and pick it up before the next wave rushes in and sweeps it back to sea. It is often a race to grab a fossil tooth before the sea can reclaim it. Seemingly all too often, the sea wins.

Off-Shore Sites

While beach sites will nearly always produce at least a few fossil teeth, there are times when no attractive "wash-ins" or "wash-outs" occur. The beach is apt to be a smooth, glistening surface of nothing but sand. Under these conditions, fossil teeth may be extremely difficult to find. While some tooth hunters simply decide to wait for the situation to change, others switch to different forms of collecting. Some, in fact, don't even bother with hunting on the beaches; they devote practically all of their effort to these other methods. They maintain that they do far better working just the off-shore sites.

One form of off-shore collecting is what is known as "drop-off dredging". This technique probably evolved when some observant tooth hunters noted the regular accumulation of heavier sea bottom material along the previously described off-shore drop-off (Figure 33). They reasoned that these deposits should contain fossil teeth So, instead of waiting for the incoming or stormy seas to toss this material up and onto the beach, they decided to reach out into the surf and haul it in. It worked.

Although there is no way of proving it one way or the other, those who prefer this type of fossil tooth collecting say they find larger and better teeth than they would prowling the beach. They contend, for example, that they are apt to find more of the much-sought-after Carcharodon megalodon teeth. Because of their size and weight, these larger teeth tend to hug the ocean bottom. They even tend to work downward into the wet sand. Consequently, the incoming waves are not apt to pick them up and toss them onto the shore. So when these drop-off dredgers rake in basketfuls of this sea bottom conglomerate, they believe their chances are better for recovering specimens of these teeth than those who wait for them to wash in.

The most frequently used piece of equipment for "drop-off dredging" is a wire mesh basket attached to a long stout handle. Some call it a "Super-Duper Shark Tooth Scooper" (Figure 39). As might be expected, there are

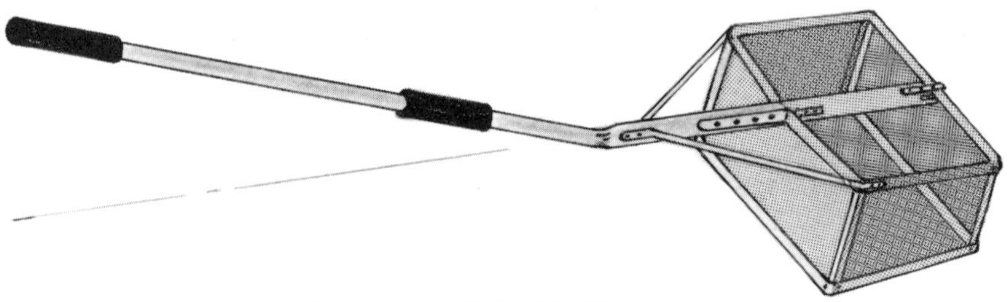

TOOTH SCOOPER

Figure 39.

numerous sizes and individual designs for these simple devices. They range from screen-covered boxes nailed together from a few scraps of wood to more durable baskets fabricated from rust-resistant aluminum. Most use a 1/4" mesh or equivalent screening such as the coated hardware cloth sold in most building supply stores. The handle is either a wooden pole, such as a rake handle, or a shaped length of aluminum tubing. The basket, which must be capable of lifting a substantial load of sand, shells and rocks, is securely fastened to the handle. Salt water, of course, is highly corrosive to ordinary iron and steel. If these metals are used, they should be coated or plated to protect them against rust.

In use, the tooth hunter wades out into the surf to within reach of the drop-off. At low tide, this may be just knee-deep water. But during a high sea with a strong on-shore wind, the water may be at least waist high. As shown in Figure 40, the scoop is extended out-

Figure 40.

ward, dropped to the sea floor, then dragged back toward shore. The dip is timed so that it is either between incoming waves or when the water is backwashing toward the sea. If done on an incoming wave, the rushing water is very apt to wash any trapped material out of the basket before it can be lifted from the bottom.

When dredging in this manner, a substantial quantity of sand is generally also picked up in the basket. Wet sand, of course, is extremely heavy. So rather than carry this unwanted extra weight through the surf then up and onto the beach, most hunters jig their baskets up and down in the sea to sift out the finer sand. It quickly washes away through the screen mesh (Figure 41).

Once collected, several different methods are used to

sort through this material. Most hunters carry it back up onto a dry, smooth part of the beach where they sort through it for any included teeth (Figure 42). Others dump it along the upper fringes of the tidal flat so that the incoming waves barely wash over it. The sweeping waters tend to fan out the material over a wide area of the beach. Any exposed teeth must then be quickly picked up before the next wave has a chance to wash them back to sea. While this method is considerably faster than hand sorting, some fossil teeth are washed back to sea and lost.

Figure 41.

Another but less elaborate type of device used to work these same sea bottom deposits is what is called a "screen" or "dip" box (Figure 43). It doesn't have a long handle on it for reaching out into the surf. Consequently, its use is generally confined to low tides and times when the sea is relatively calm. The collector wades out to the drop-off where the "screen" box is used to scoop up sea bottom material. In much the same way as done with the scoop, the box is then jigged up and down in the water to wash away the finer sands. While some tooth hunters prefer to go through their recovered material without leaving the sea, most carry it back up onto the beach where they or a partner carefully sort through it for any included fossil teeth.

Figure 42.

Another interesting and sometimes particularly rewarding method of off-shore tooth collecting is to use a skin-diving or Scuba (self contained underwater breathing apparatus) gear (Figure 44). When the sea is particularly calm and the near-shore waters clear and free of churned up sand, a swimmer using a face-mask, snorkel and swim fins can cruise along the edge of the shallow

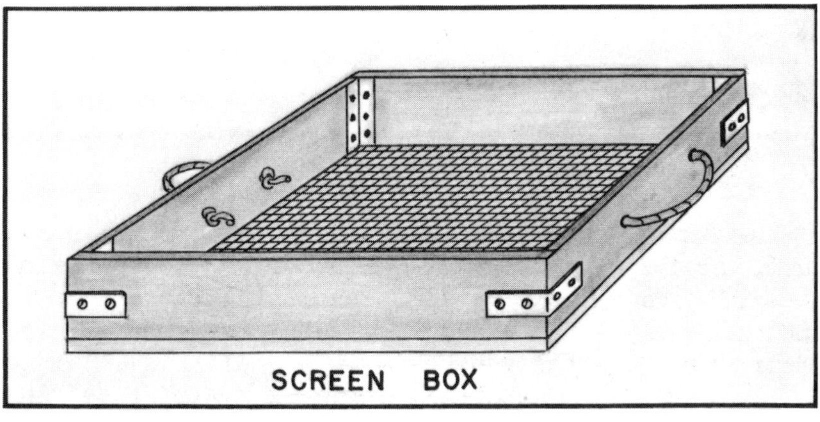

Figure 43.

water drop-off looking for fossil teeth. On occasions when the water is particularly cold, a wet suit may be required.

When skin-diving, most of the searching is done close to shore in water that is only a few feet deep. Some divers, however, prefer to venture further out in search of exposed shell, rock and fossil beds. Like the beach itself, there are times the sea floor is almost entirely an uninterrupted smooth, sand bottom. At other times, however, beds of heavier objects are sometimes exposed. From these, some extremely valuable finds have been made. From the Venice beaches, ridges of this favorable material are apt to be found 200 to 400 yards off-shore in 15 to 25 feet of water. It is reported that one particularly skilled underwater collector, working these deposits, has recovered nearly 500 Carcharodon teeth. Their retail value has been estimated to be over $25,000.

Figure 44.

When snorkel or Scuba hunting in either the shallow surf, or further off-shore, hunters very seldom find a fossil tooth clearly outlined against the sandy bottom. Instead, only a hard-to-detect corner or an edge may be protruding from the sand or from a shell pile. A slow, careful, methodical search along a short section of shore line is often far more productive than a rapid skimming of a longer stretch of sea bottom.

Inland Sites

In the distant past, the land that is now the Florida peninsula was flooded by the seas for long periods of time (Figures 3 and 4). Many generations of sea life lived and perished in these waters, their remains settling to the bottom. In some cases, they were buried, then fossilized under subsequent deposits of sediment.

Today, some of these marine deposits of former times are above sea level, where they are subject to the erosive actions of the winds and rains. Remains of ancient fish and other sea life are continually being freed from their former burial site. Sharks' teeth are apt to be included; and because they have not been subject to the abrasive actions of the ocean's sands, inland fossil finds are often far better preserved than those from the sea.

Among Florida's inland locations where such ancient sea bottom deposits are exposed on the land surface are numerous sites in and around Venice. Generally, the most favorable of these are (1) flats where most of the vegetation has been cleared away exposing the bare soil, and (2) spoil banks (Figure 45) created by such excavation work as drainage ditches. Land cleared for trailer parks, housing developments and similar building projects are among such locations.

The best time for collecting from inland sites is generally after a heavy rain. The running waters tend to wash away the loose, softly packed sands, exposing the more difficult to move fossils. After a heavy rain,

Figure 45.

experienced hunters look along drainage ditch spoil banks or vegetation-free banks sloping down into ravines and canals. When searching such banks, a short handled garden tool with curved tines (Figure 46) is useful for probing through the sandy loam to locate buried fossils. A shovel and screen box are also helpful. Sand dug from the bank is sifted through the screen box to sort out any included fossils.

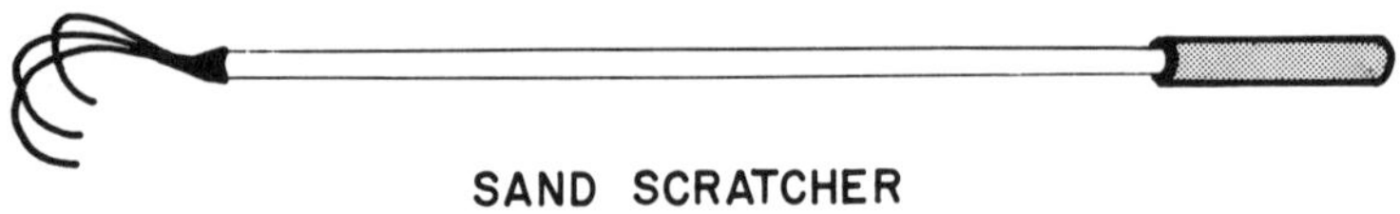

Figure 46.

When a fossil tooth is found at an inland site, it is generally advisable to concentrate more effort in the immediate vicinity of such a find. Often one fossil is from a nearby deposit that may contain many more.

Another inland form of fossil-bearing deposit is what some call a "shell bed." Very much like the previously described wash-in and wash-out deposits, these are buried beds of whole and broken shells, stones, fossils and fossil fragments. But instead of being related to today's sea levels and coast lines, these beds were laid down in the past when the seas flooded more of the land. Such "shell beds" may be well inland or relatively close to today's coast line.

On days when the collecting beaches are particularly barren, shell beds can sometimes be a tooth hunter's salvation. They can turn what might otherwise be a non-productive day into a successful one.

In Figure 47, a typical shell bed near the coast line is shown. Such beds are often located by an exposed "outcrop" where the land slopes downward from a higher elevation. The sloping edges of ravines or steep banks are good places to look for such beds.

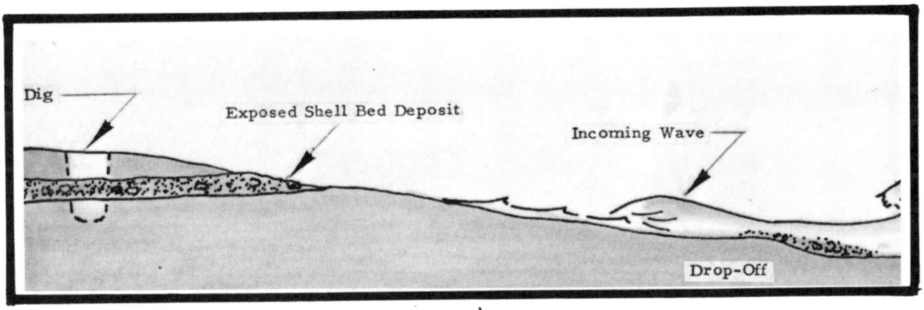

Figure 47.

While a number of different approaches are used by tooth hunters to sort this shell bed material for fossil teeth, a screened box (Figure 43) is probably the most popular method. Shovel loads of material from the bed are heaped into the dip box. Then when it has been filled, it is taken to the nearest water for washing. The loose sand is jigged away, then the remaining bits and pieces sorted for any included sharks' teeth.

Whether it be inland "shell beds", off-shore dredging or any one of the other forms of collecting, those who have tried shark tooth hunting have found there are far more opportunities for finding attractive specimens than are at first apparent. Collecting can be successfully done at almost any time of the year and under nearly any kind of weather conditions. In fact, bad weather is often more favorable than good. New materials are apt to be thrown up on the beaches, particularly the prized Carcharodon megalodon teeth. Heavy storm rains also tend to uncover still buried fossils in spoil banks and on fossil-bearing sandy flats.

While the beach and its attractive environment will

undoubtedly continue to be the favorite collecting ground for most, don't overlook these other hunting opportunities. They just may substantially improve your results.

AFTER THE HUNT - THE COLLECTION

While hunting fossilized teeth is in itself an intriguing pastime, all collectors are ultimately forced to decide what to do with their finds. Some, who pick up just a few, put them in a small plastic pill vial or small glass container which they display on a shelf at home. Others take a few of the more attractive specimens and hang them from charm bracelets or necklaces. A number are also given to children to take to school for "show and tell." But for many, their interest carries them into more serious collecting and displaying of their results. They ultimately sort, classify, then prepare attractive glass-covered display cases to show

Figure 48.

their finds. Usually they are arranged by shark species, with only the larger and more perfect specimens being shown. Typically, commercial 12"x8"x1" glass-lid display trays are used for this purpose (Figure 48). These flat, thin boxes, which are also commonly used for insect, plant life, mineral and similar displays, are usually available in hobby shops. The fossil teeth are neatly arranged on the soft cotton bedding with identifying labels added as desired. When the window-glass cover is in place, it usually exerts enough downward pressure to hold the teeth in place.

Other more elaborate methods are, of course, also available for displaying these attractive prehistoric fossils. They do much to enhance the appearance of a collection.

While not starting out with the intent to collect for profit, some hobbyists eventually acquire so many sharks' teeth that they ultimately decide to sell all or some of them. With the immense popularity created in a large part by the book and movie "Jaws," there has been a steady market for good-quality shark's teeth. While broken and particularly small specimens are of negligible value, prices of $.50 and even more are often asked for good to very good 1" to 1-1/2" long specimens.

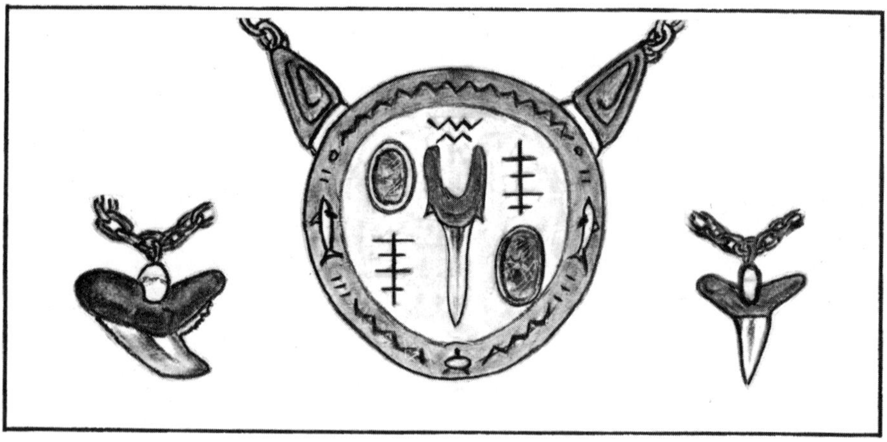

Figure 49.

Such undamaged teeth are in greatest demand by the jewelry trade, where they find attractive application in charm bracelets, necklaces, earrings and sililar adornments (Figure 49). But by comparison, these are very moderate prices compared to those asked for the even larger fossil teeth. For good-sized Carcharodon megalodon and extinct Mako shark teeth, asking prices of from

$25 to $100 each are not unusual. Outstanding specimens range well above this, with prices approaching $200 attached to very large, unbroken, finely detailed ones. These are the unusually rare specimens that are most often found by those who devote a great deal of hunting time and effort to this pastime.

Before deciding it might be an easy way to make a living, remember it is only the more attractive, better-preserved specimens that bring good prices. The more commonly found smaller sizes and chipped specimens are usually not worth more than $.05 to $.10 each. It is almost certain that the revenue from an average full day's tooth hunt will invariably be far below the legal minimum wage for any regular job. It's not the potential revenue that attracts a majority of people to this pastime. Instead, it is the appeal of the hunt, the attractiveness of the beach environment, and the fascination generated by these interesting fossils themselves.

For those who plan to use part of their collection in jewelry or similar displays, there is a choice between showing the teeth in a natural, "as found," condition and working on them to improve their finish and appearance. Some ardent collectors believe it is totally inappropriate to alter a fossil tooth from the state in which it was found. They argue it distorts the authenticity of the tooth as a fossil. On the other hand, those who want to display them as a part of an attractive piece of jewelry contend they should display as much of the tooth's natural, unblemished beauty as possible. Consequently, this latter group refurbishes their specimens to reinstate much of the tooth's original luster and ivory-like appearance.

One of the simplest and most effective tools for improving a fossil tooth's outward appearance is a sheep's wool buffing wheel. Attachments of this sort, that fit most home workshop 1/4" and larger electric drills, are widely available in hardware and large department stores (Figure 50). The tooth is held against the rotating wool

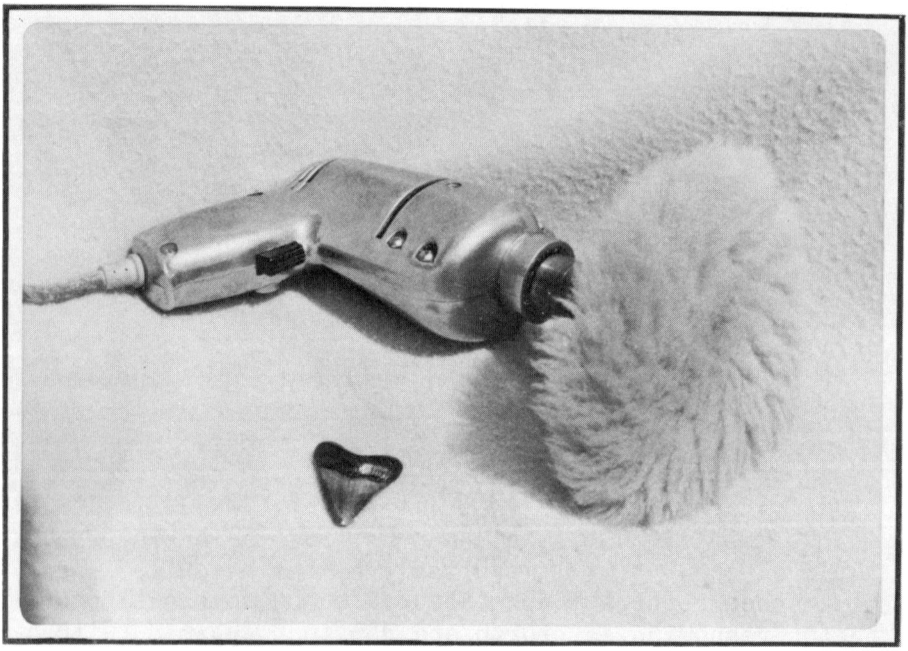

Figure 50.

wheel, which tends to buff out slight surface scratches and blemishes. These color-dulling imperfections generally occur when the tooth is scuffed along the sandy bottom by the sea. While such polishing tends to restore the luster and sheen to the enamel part of the tooth, it only slightly improves the appearance of the more porous, bony base. This usually darker part of the tooth generally contains many pin size holes which are typical of most bony structures. This more irregular surface cannot be expected to reach the same high luster as the denser, more ivory-like enamel.

To further enhance the tooth's color and finish, jewelry-grade specimens are often also sprayed with a thin, clear protective film of an acrylic plastic such as Krylon's No. 1303. These crystal clear aerosol sprays can be obtained in most art supply stores. Before application, however, the tooth is first buffed to a high luster. A thin coat is then sprayed on and allowed to dry. This is followed by rebuffing. Besides giving additional luster to the enamel, the acrylic coating is particularly effective in toning up the tooth's bony base. It tends to darken otherwise dull greys to ebony blacks and faded browns to more attractive copper-like colors. The color transformation from a dull, nondescript finish to a deep, more ivory-like luster is often quite pronounced in some specimens.

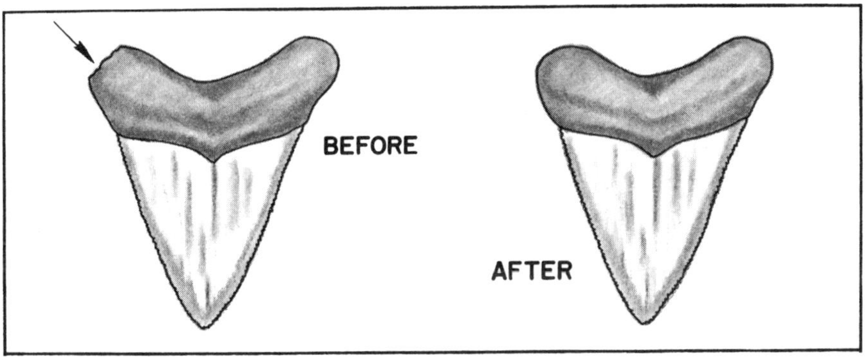

Figure 51.

Another restoration action taken by some collectors is the reshaping of broken and chipped specimens with a grinding wheel or file. This must be done with a great deal of care, particularly on the crown of the tooth. Too much cutting on this part can result in part of the outer enamel chipping away, exposing the less attractive underlying root. When this happens, the tooth's appearance is hurt rather than improved. The bone-like base, however, is more tolerant of grinding and filing. A grinding wheel, for instance, can be used to reshape the chipped corner of the base, giving it a well-contoured, smooth, more natural configuration. By progressively sanding off the reshaped surface with finer and finer grades of sandpaper, the original imperfection can be almost completely eliminated. Figure 51 shows an example of such work. This refinishing is usually confined to the larger, potentially more valuable tooth specimens, not the normal run of smaller fossil teeth.

While the small, dark shark's teeth lend themselves to attractive necklace, earring and bracelet applications, the large Carcharodon megalodon fossils are not as adaptable to jewelry use. Teeth up to about 3" in length find use in silver belt buckle mountings and as a pendant in some necklaces. Above this size, the tooth is usually too big and massive to fit such applicatins. Those who are fortunate enough to have one or more of these more awesome prehistoric shark's teeth often choose to display them apart from the rest of their collection. Most shell shops and rock shops carry several different types of display mounts that will accommodate these fossils. One popular mount, for example, is a small tripod with retainers on the legs to hold the display. It works much like a scaled-down version of an artist's easel, but it is only one of many to choose from. If you are fortunate enough to own one of these relatively rare giant shark's teeth, by all means display it for all to admire. And if you don't, why not try finding one? The restless sea, the churning surf and the constantly changing tides continue to challenge those who love and enjoy the beach. And to the delight of many, a vast array of sharks teeth continue to be tossed up onto the sandy shores for them to find. Why not join in the fun?

OTHER READING

Title	Author
A Comprehensive Geology	Amadeus W. Grabau
Adventures in Marine Collecting	Robert P. L. Straughan
Basic Concepts of Historical Geology	Edgar W. Spencer
Blue Meridian, The Search for the Great White Shark	Peter Matthiessen
Danger - Shark!	Jean Campbell Butler
Dictionary of Sharks	Patricia E. Pope
Essentials of Earth History	Wm. Lee Stokes
Fossil Sharks: A Pictorial Review	Gerard R. Case
Fossil Vertebrates - Beach and Bank Collecting for Amateurs	M. C. Thomas
Guide to Marine Fishes	Alfred Perlmutter
Kelley's Guide to Fossil Sharks	K. V. Kelley, Jr.
McClane's New Standard Fishing Encyclopedia	Albert Jules McClane
Monster Teeth of Chesapeake Bay	Ellsworth Boyd, "Skin Diver," Jan., 1975
Myth and Maneater - The Story of the Shark	David Kenyon Webster
Sharks and Rays	Spencer Wilkie Tinker and Charles J. DeLuca
Sharks: Wolves of the Sea	Nathaniel T. Kenny, "National Geographic," Feb., 1968
Shark Safari	Captain Hal Scharp
Sharks, Skates and Rays	Gilbert, Matheusen and Rall
Size of the Great White Shark (Carcharodon)	John E. Randall, "Science," July 13, 1973
Tales Told by Fossils	Carroll Lane Fenton
The Day of the Dinosaur	L. Sprague de Camp and Catherine C. de Camp
The Life of Sharks	Paul Budker
The Shark: Splendid Savage of the Sea	Jacques-Yves Cousteau and Philippe Cousteau
Vertebrate Paleontology	Alfred S. Romer
Wandering Lands and Animals	Edwin H. Colbert

FOSSIL SHARK'S TEETH

Various size, quality and shark species fossil teeth, primarily collected in Florida, are available through "Natural Science Research". Most are from Miocene deposits dating back 12 to 28 million years.

To obtain a Price List of currently available fossil teeth, please send a self-addressed, stamped envelope to:

Natural Science Research
2307 Manchester Road
Ann Arbor, Michigan 48104